CONTINENTAL CONGRESS COURAGEOUS

The Delegates at York Town, PA
1777–1778

CONTINENTAL CONGRESS COURAGEOUS

The Delegates at York Town, PA
1777–1778

JOHN F. RAUHAUSER, JR.
HELEN MILLER GOTWALT
ELIZABETH L. RAUHAUSER STEIN
THOMAS L. SCHAEFER

This book is dedicated to those who dare to dream of unity, justice, and peace, and to those who have the courage to make those dreams come true.

E. Stein

Project management, page composition, art rendering, and printing by TechBooks

© 2001 The York Bicentennial Commission, Inc.
Printed in the United States of America
ISBN 0-9714587-0-7

TABLE OF CONTENTS

Beyond the vignettes and images found here, this volume also provides an interesting object of reflection into a person's dreams and an era of American culture now passed.

The Hon. John F. Rauhauser, Jr., more than any other, assembled and pled the case that York, Pennsylvania, and not Philadelphia or New York City bore the right to claim title of the First Capital of the United States. His reasoning derived from the precedent terminology found within the Articles of Confederation, which were both drafted and passed here in York. While, most certainly, Congress met in other places before arriving in York, and while, most certainly, its members had begun to act in concert to build the legislation of a new nation, as Rauhauser maintained, the style of term "United States of America" had, arguably, not been evoked, nor had the fledgling states agreed within a legal document to join in exactly such a manner.

John Rauhauser's vision of York's Revolutionary Era importance extended beyond the concept of the city being the First Capital. He, and others, had a more tangible goal in mind. Rauhauser was a leader in what became a community effort to fund the reconstruction of York County's first courthouse, the building where the Continental Congress met between September 30, 1777, and June 27, 1778. This dream came to fruition with the replica's dedication on May 1, 1976. The ceremony was York's focal event during celebration of America's Bicentennial.

A number of York Countians have been generally aware of John Rauhauser's involvement with the First Capital claim and the Colonial Courthouse reconstruction, but far fewer knew that he had been working to complete another project. It was yet another dream that focused attention on York's importance during the Revolution. Moreover, this project was envisioned to reinforce the significance and humanity of the delegates who met, planned, and regularly argued within York County's first courthouse.

Rauhauser's dream was a book meant to breathe a sense of life back within the courthouse's stark walls. It was to be a collection of "life sketches," one for each delegate who came to York during the time that Congress sat here. Rauhauser knew that the lives of certain delegates were well recorded, but he also knew that others who deserved the title "Founding Father" had long ago drifted into obscurity. Being a judge, community leader, and family man, he could only work on his dream sporadically. He amassed many notes, visited many places, and shared his vision of the completed manuscript with his family and certain close friends and acquaintances. Alas, John F. Rauhauser, Jr., died in 1993 before his dream was fulfilled.

As he neared the end of his days, he was most anxious to ensure that his vision would not end with him. He found a willing ally in his friend and trusted colleague Helen Miller Gotwalt. The two were long-standing friends, and because of her teaching and writing experience, Rauhauser knew she was worthy of completing the task. Most applicably, Gotwalt had previously written the story of York County's first courthouse building; therefore, she was already familiar with the people and events that brought prominence to what, prior to 1777, had been merely a small county courthouse. Gotwalt's volume, *Crucible of a New Nation,* was published in 1977 by the county's Bicentennial Commission. Its story is a fascinating one, for Gotwalt was able to weave the history of the structure itself, the community, the personalities of the congressional delegates, and the forming of the Articles of Confederation into an evocative, informative narrative. Alas, Helen Miller Gotwalt died in 1997 before she could complete Rauhauser's manuscript.

The next person to take up the challenge was Judge Rauhauser's youngest daughter, Elizabeth

Stein. She well knew her father's desires and enthusiasms, and as a busy schoolteacher and mother of three, she worked to fit in the time required to do the book justice. She and her family began to plan their vacations around visits to graveyards, historic homes, and repositories holding documents related to those delegates who were lesser known than Samuel Adams or Henry Laurens. Many images were assembled and reams of old notes placed in a semblance of order, so that, finally, the work dreamt of by Rauhauser, shaped and further narrated by Gotwalt, and fleshed out and reorganized by Betty Stein, could be brought to publication.

At that juncture, it was decided to engage professional assistance so that the missing segments of research could be filled in and the manuscript reviewed and edited to reflect a single voice. And that is the work in hand. As a point of historiography, it is important to note the "voice" of this writing. Most of it was either drafted or completed by two authors who were schooled during the 1920s and 1940s. (Indeed, Helen Miller Gotwalt was both English teacher and drama coach to John Rauhauser when he was a student in the York City schools.) It was therefore decided to complete the balance of the writing in the tenor and the rhetorical style set by them. Academic readers will immediately note that much has changed since that era of writing and research was *en vogue*. Yet, this writing is well as it should be, for it was completed as it was *meant* to be by John Rauhauser and Helen Miller Gotwalt, and

in doing so, it serves as a testimonial to the type of prose and the vigor of emotion that era of Americans reflected in their appreciation of America's past. Both Rauhauser and Gotwalt wished to capture the humanity—for better and for worse—of the sixty-four delegates who, some reluctantly, struggled into York to thrash out our Constitution's precursor. As the shape of this project was fairly well developed before Rauhauser's death, it was also clear that what he envisioned was not a collection of definitive, highly documented biographies but, rather, a gathering of vignettes that illustrated the range and dimensions of those who huddled through the bleak winter of 1777–1778 while attempting to weld together a nation's political framework.

To close this note, I'll draw on an analogy of a relay team determined to run their collective best. It has been a pleasure to be the person running the fourth leg of this long race, who was chosen, finally, to carry the baton across the finish line. In our race, Rauhauser's start-off the line was solid, and he set a good pace. The baton passes to Gotwalt and Stein were clean, and the finish line was cleared with renewed vigor! Yet, the ultimate winners in this venture are those who make up York's community, for now, one more contribution that narrates our county's rich heritage has been brought before the public.

Thomas L. Schaefer
December 2000

AN HISTORIAN'S PERSPECTIVE

While many York Countians know that the Continental Congress met here for nine months, many readers from farther afield may not be aware of York's significance during the American Revolution. Moreover, many may not recall why Congress came to York in the first place. A very small, inland Pennsylvania village, York was an unlikely place for Congress to gather, but in great measure, that is precisely why Congress did come here.

The summer campaigns of 1777 had not gone well for the Continental army. A command under British General John Burgoyne had swept south from Canada with the intent of splitting the northern colonies in two. Having previously driven Washington's forces away from New York City and through New Jersey, Sir William Howe's substantial force launched a campaign to capture Philadelphia, which they succeeded in doing after victories at Brandywine, Paoli, and Germantown. George Washington's star had slipped toward its nadir. His army had lost men, equipment, and most of its morale, and the Continental Congress had lost its seat of government, Independence Hall.

When the British first pressed on Philadelphia, it was shockingly clear that Congress had to abandon the city. But, where should they relocate? The immediate thought was to move inland and put as much distance as possible between themselves and the Redcoats. Locations in Chester, Bucks, or Philadelphia Counties were still too close for comfort, but Lancaster was more promising. As a Pennsylvania "back country" market town, founded in 1721, Lancaster had a courthouse in which business could be conducted, and it was a community sufficiently sized to host, albeit modestly, the number and tastes of the delegates and the remaining entourage that made up our fledgling government's offices.

Congress convened in Lancaster for one day. During that session, they made a key decision—as comfortable as Lancaster was for a meeting venue, it was still uncomfortably close to Philadelphia and the British. The sheer distance and the line of the Schuylkill River afforded some protection, but perhaps crossing beyond inland Pennsylvania's most substantial physical barrier, the Susquehanna River, would provide better protection.

With that, Congress again adjourned, now resolved to meet in York Town "on Tuesday next at 10 o'clock." Indeed, the nearly one-mile-wide Susquehanna River would offer far better protection. No substantial body of hostile forces could cross that river either secretly or quickly. That, coupled with York being an additional one or two days of travel beyond Lancaster, gave Congress a sense that they were, in the words of delegate James Duane, "sufficiently retired" so they "could deliberate without fear of interruption." Another factor, however, was also at play. Pennsylvania's State Assembly was already meeting in Lancaster. Therefore, had Congress remained, things would have become more crowded than cozy, and so Congress retired to York.

What sort of place was it to which Congress had sufficiently retired? York's streets and building lots were plotted in 1741, thirty-five years before the Declaration of Independence was first read in Philadelphia, approximately ninety miles to York's east. That city, being William Penn's capital and major port, dominated much of the colony's development throughout its first fifty years. As settlers continued to move into the back country of Penn's thickly wooded land grant, a ring of other, far smaller towns, such as Chester, Newtown, and Germantown, began serving as a second generation of social, economic, and political focal points.

By the late 1730's, sufficient numbers of people had pushed west beyond the Susquehanna River toward the Blue Mountain range—and toward what then remained Indian territory. This Trans-Susquehanna region was designated as Hellam Township in 1739. A vast space comprising what is now York, Adams, and part of Cumberland Counties, it fell under the legal jurisdiction of Lancaster County, itself formed in 1729. This was Pennsylvania's frontier.

York became the social and economic focal point for much of the Trans-Susquehanna soon after its founding in 1741. It was surveyed under the direction of Thomas Cookson on behalf of John, Thomas, and Richard Penn, who had since become the proprietors of their father's colony. They saw the necessity for opening a market town in the Trans-Susquehanna, and Cookson, Lancaster County's deputy surveyor, saw the benefits of placing it at the intersection of the Codorus Creek and the Monocacy Trail. His site was in the midst of a fertile, well-watered limestone valley. York's street grid, modeled after Philadelphia's, stretched in part along a low rise, assuring good drainage and fresh breezes. Its lots fit neatly beside a straight run of the Codorus, which then bent acutely to frame the town's northern approach.

Applications for twenty-three lots were registered by November, 1741. By 1749, sixty-three dwellings had been built or were still under construction, and two churches stood. Also in 1749, York became the governmental seat for the newly created York County. By 1754, when the first courthouse was completed (in which Congress would later meet), approximately 180 dwellings were standing and another thirty under construction. Those figures are contained within a detailed letter written by George Stevenson, who resurveyed York's lots. He mentions a growing village, but one not without problems. He noted that the population was primarily German-speaking, and that no wood-lots or pasturelands were handy. It would be difficult to state precisely what configuration of town awaited the congressional delegates in 1777, but a survey compiled five years later at the Revolution's close lists York as having 293 houses and a population of 1,779, including representatives of a diversity of occupations.

A later document, the U.S. Federal Direct Tax of 1798, yields a very precise picture of York's built environment twenty years following Congress' visit. York then held 385 completed dwellings. Of these, 264 were wooden, 98 were brick, 14 were stone, and 9 were half-timber. One-story wooden structures comprised 44.41% of the total, or nearly *half* of what stood in York—not in 1777, but in 1798. Many of those structures were of modest dimensions as well. For example, 53 of York's 385 houses, or 13.77%, measured approximately 16 by 16 feet.

In 1777, York had no pavement, no cobblestoned streets, little in the way of high-style food and drink, an economy primarily rooted in a barter system practiced by German speakers, and very little in the way of entertainment. Congress most certainly was trading a fair number of creature comforts available in Philadelphia, four or five days journey eastward, for the safety that "Little York on the Codorus" afforded. Such were the times and conditions that "tried men's souls." Still, as one will read, these congressional delegates were sufficiently courageous to meet such adversities while they struggled to forge the bonds of a new nation. Here are some insights into their lives.

Thomas L. Schaefer
December 2000

CONTRIBUTORS

JOHN F. RAUHAUSER, JR.

Senior Judge Rauhauser was a person of diverse interests and abilities. In addition to his love of law and history, he was an adept artist, a theatre enthusiast, a community leader, a quick wit, and a grand story teller. It was his idea to tell the stories of the Patriots who found themselves in York Town so many years ago. A graduate of William Penn Senior High School and Ursinus College, he was awarded his law degree by the University of Pennsylvania in 1948. He practiced law in York between 1949 and 1982, when he was elected to a judgeship. He had also served as the county's solicitor and was District Attorney between 1966 and 1969. He became a senior judge and served in that capacity until his retirement in 1992.

During World War II, Rauhauser saw service in both the army and the navy. He was very active in the York community and in his church. He received numerous awards for his contributions, including an honorary Doctorate of Humane Letters from York College of Pennsylvania. In 1978, he was named to William Penn Senior High's Hall of Fame. His deep interest in York's past led him to the presidency of the York County Bicentennial Commission. He also was appointed by Governor Richard Thornburgh to Pennsylvania's Commonwealth Commission for the Bicentennial and was honored by the Philadelphia Chamber of Commerce and the Daughters of the American Revolution.

HELEN MILLER GOTWALT

As an educator, Helen Miller Gotwalt shaped the minds and interests of countless students during her decades of teaching at Hannah Penn Junior High School and William Penn Senior High School. John F. Rauhauser, Jr., was one of them. Their relationship blossomed from student/teacher to research colleagues and ultimately, to life-long friends—their interests were strikingly similar. Gotwalt came to York's schools after graduating from Shippensburg State Teachers College in 1925. She headed Hannah Penn's English department for 23 years and was deeply involved in York's theatrical world. She also became one of the region's pioneers in developing educational television programming for youth.

Gotwalt loved combining history and drama. She wrote more than 300 children's plays, and she produced and directed many of them for local TV and radio. She also wrote plays for the Traveling Theatre. For her many accomplishments, she was named a Distinguished Pennsylvanian, and in 1988, York College of Pennsylvania awarded her an honorary Doctorate of Humane Letters. For the county's Bicentennial celebration, she wrote *Crucible of a New Nation,* a book telling the fascinating story of York's colonial-era court house in which Congress met. Gotwalt was a natural successor to continue her former student's work.

Elizabeth L. Rauhauser Stein

The youngest of Judge Rauhauser's three daughters, Elizabeth "Betty" Stein was witness to the colleague-ship her father shared with Helen Miller Gotwalt. During the declining years of them both, she began taking an active role in helping with the completion of the research and the manuscript for this work. She also shared the vision her father had for this project. Stein even drew in her husband, Douglas, and their three daughters, whose vacations often came to be focused on researching information about the delegates.

Stein graduated from Central High School and did her undergraduate work at Bloomsburg State College. In 1984, she received a Masters in Special Education from Western Maryland College. She also holds a Supervisory Certificate from that institution. For five years, she taught special education for the Lincoln Intermediate Unit #12, and since 1983, Stein has served as a learning support teacher at the elementary level for the Spring Grove School District. She has also been involved with the district's Swim Club, Spring Grove Music Boosters, and the Spring Grove Athletic Association. Like her father, she has taken an active role in community affairs, including church-related activities and in the York/Adams County Special Olympics program. Stein has served as a board member for the York County Bicentennial Commission and currently holds the office of secretary.

Thomas L. Schaefer

A 1969 graduate of William Penn Senior High School, Schaefer went on to study clarinet at the Peabody Conservatory of Music, playing professionally for a number of years. He later spent a year in England as an archaeologist. He did his undergraduate degree in History at Susquehanna University and also completed course work in Fine Arts and Architectural History at Oxford University and the University of London. His Masters Degree in American Studies is from Penn State. He has been employed in the fields of historic preservation, architectural history, oral history, and archival management, and he has studied York County's history since 1979.

Schaefer was an academic administrator at Penn State York for 13 years, where he also designed and taught more than 50 courses and touring programs based on local history and Gettysburg Campaign themes. Since 1998, he has been a writer and historical consultant, and he continues to teach, lecture, and offer study tours privately. He is the author of *York County at 250: The Patterns of Our Past*, written as part of the celebration of the county's 250th anniversary. Beyond his academic writings, Schaefer's works include *A Touring Guide to Dauphin County* and the forthcoming *An Unexplored Heritage*, a book examining the interconnections of law and history in York County.

ACKNOWLEDGMENTS

The Bicentennial Commission would like to thank the following people for their help during the preparation of this title:

Board members: Allan Anger, Norman Callahan, Kip Dunlap, Wallace Dunlap, William Falkler, Mark Frankel, Voni Grimes, Ken Hoffman, Margie Rauhauser Marsh, John Marsh, Marion McAfee, Daisy Myers, Angela Orwig, Dorothy Rauhauser, Kathy Rauhauser, Landon Reisinger, Jim Rudisill, Frank Shaffer, Barry Shepp, Luther Sowers, Kevin Springman, Douglas Stein, Elizabeth Stein, Patricia Stentz, Robert Wolfgang.

Book Committee Members: Frank Shaffer, Alan Anger, Elizabeth Stein, and Douglas Stein.

Historians: Landon Reisinger and James Rudisill, for providing historical information and reviewing the manuscript for its historical accuracy.

The Stein family: Douglas, Jacquelyn, Jessica, Jennifer, for their patience, love, and support, and for spending many summer vacations traveling to obtain information from archives, historical societies, and old graveyards.

The Rauhauser family: Dorothy Rauhauser, Kathy Rauhauser, and Marjory Rauhauser Marsh for their love, assistance, and support throughout this project.

Judge John Uhler: for his assistance at the beginning of this project.

Nancy Rudisill, York Graphics: for her perseverance and coordination at the onset of this project.

TechBooks: David Smith, Kevin Bradley, Denise Keller, Candice Carta, and Roark Mitzell.

P.H. Glatfelter Company: our thanks to the company and its employees for donating the paper.

Our thanks also goes out to all of the people, too numerous to name, from historical societies, archives, museums, national parks, libraries, cemeteries, and churches, as well as the descendants of delegates who provided assistance, guidance, and information for this book.

CONNECTICUT

Dyer, Eliphalet
Hosmer, Titus
Huntington, Samuel
Law, Richard
Sherman, Roger
Williams, William
Wolcott, Oliver

ELIPHALET DYER

BIRTH: Windham, Connecticut
　　　September 14, 1721

DEATH: Windham, Connecticut
　　　May 13, 1807

COLONY: Connecticut

EDUCATION: Yale

PROFESSION: Lawyer, Merchant, Politician

AT YORK TOWN: September 30, 1777–
　　　　　January 31, 1778
　　　　　February 1, 1778–
　　　　　April 3, 1778

When, along with Roger Sherman and Silas Deane, Eliphalet Dyer was elected to the first Continental Congress in 1774, he was a fifty-three-year-old, seasoned politician, a successful lawyer, a wealthy land-owner, and a businessman. He had worked his way up the ladder of Connecticut politics, he advanced himself in the Militia, and he was one of four Chief Justices of the Supreme Court, a delegate to the Colonial Assembly, and a member of Colonial Council.

His pet project was the establishment of a new colony on the west bank of the Susquehanna River, on land claimed by Connecticut but owned and controlled by Pennsylvania. As agent of the Susquehanna Company, he spent six months in London in 1763 in a vain attempt to obtain a royal charter for the proposed colony. Although his mission was a business failure, the trip gave him first-hand knowledge about the workings of Parliament and the Court of St. James. He was also able to assess the temper of the English toward America, which convinced him that, by 1774, "they have now drawn the Sword; in order to execute their plan of subduing America, and I imagine they will not sheathe it, but that next Summer will decide the Fate of America." He was right.

When the same trio—Roger Sherman, Silas Deane, and Dyer—were elected to the Second Continental Congress in 1775, the "shot heard around the world" had already been fired. The

"Leathern conveniency" belonging to Silas Deane, in which the three men traveled, was greeted by brass bands and throngs of cheering people along the way. Dyer interpreted this as "a strong testimony of the Spirit and Unanimity of the people."

During these Philadelphia sessions, he put his political skills to work by recommending Joseph Trumbull, son of his good friend and also Dyer's future son-in-law, for the post of Secretary to General Washington, whom he found "discreet and virtuous, no harum-scarum, ranting, swearing fellow, but sober, steady and calm." Although his recommendation failed, he did succeed in having the young man appointed as Commissary General. Like many other 18th century politicians, he used his position to favor his relatives, friends, and constituents. His son, Thomas, and his nephew, Ebeneezer Gary, were appointed captains, and Jonathan Trumbull, Jr., was named Paymaster General of the army. In defense of his patronage activities, he vowed that he never recommended anyone unqualified or harmful to the service. Nor could it ever be said that he neglected his duties or weakened his conviction regarding the expediency and necessity for complete independence from Britain.

Dyer did not return to Philadelphia until 1777, when he was forced, along with the rest of Congress, to flee—first to Lancaster, and then to York Town—in September of that year. Once established at York Town, he was an ardent supporter of the Articles of Confederation, participating vigorously in all the debates. Unfortunately, among his skills as a politician, he had been denied the gift of oratory. He was called "boring, tedious, peevish and loquacious" by many in his captive audiences.

In his letters, however, these qualities are not apparent. They tend to reflect more of his personal warmth, sincerity, and abiding dedication to his country. The bulk of his York Town correspondence was directed to his son-in-law, Joseph Trumbull, whose absence from his post as Commissionary General, during a time when the army was in desperate need of a steady, well-organized line of supplies, was of great personal concern. The young man, on the pretext of ill health, was actually "sulking in his tent" over an inadvertent insult to his father: President Laurens had addressed a circular letter from Congress to the Speaker of the Assembly instead of to Governor Trumbull.

After suggesting a cure for jaundice (a decoction of soot with the yolk of an egg) and many assurances of respect for the Trumbull name, Dyer spelled out a patriot's duty:

> The security of our country in no measure ought to be neglected on account of any real or supposed affronts or injuries whatever. I never would have seen this place and sacrificed my interest, and the comforts of my family, had not I valued my country, and held myself superior to reproach.

Although Dyer suffered frequent and often severe reproach throughout his public life, he never deviated from that principle. By the time of his retirement, he had lost much of what was near and dear to him. His son, Oliver, had died of consumption. His son-in-law, Joseph Trumbull, had also passed away, as had his wife and eldest son, Thomas. During the last years of his life, being denied the comfort of his family, his personal needs were supplied by three servants.

The sharp-tongued John Adams said of him;

> Dyer is long-winded, and round-about, obscure and cloudy, very talkative and very tedious . . . YET . . . [and this is how Eliphalet Dyer deserves to be remembered] . . . "an honest man [who] means and judges well."

IN MEMORY OF
The Honorable
Titus Hosmer Esq.
who died August 4th
D. 1780
in the Fourty Fourth
Year of his Age

TITUS HOSMER

BIRTH: West Hartford, Connecticut
1736

DEATH: Middletown, Connecticut
August 4, 1780

COLONY: Connecticut

EDUCATION: Yale College

PROFESSION: Lawyer, Politician, Judge

AT YORK TOWN: June 23, 1778–
June 27, 1778

Titus Hosmer was a man of breeding and intelligence, with a talent for reasoning and a taste for good literature. He commenced the study and practice of law in Middletown, Connecticut, and in 1761, a year after he was admitted to the Bar, he married Lydia Lord, with whom he had seven children, one of whom grew up to be Chief Justice of the Supreme Court of Connecticut.

The Hosmer home was a gathering place for cultivated people, and his library of more than two-hundred volumes was available to friends and neighbors. He was a genial host, enjoyed the company of intelligent men and women, and earned the reputation of being one of Connecticut's most able and distinguished legal personalities. Their faith in him was reflected by his successful elections to numerous local offices.

Hosmer was elected as a representative to the Connecticut General Assembly in 1773 and repeatedly re-elected until 1778. He served as House Speaker in 1776 and 1778. He then served as Assistant until his death in 1780. No idle man, he also served in his State Senate between 1778 and 1780. Titus Hosmer is credited with greatly influencing the legislature to enact strong measures against Great Britain.

In 1778, he was elected to Continental Congress and took his seat in York Town just four days before its adjournment to Philadelphia. His arrival had been eagerly anticipated by Samuel Huntington, who urged him to be present by June 1st. Hosmer was unable to report for duty, however, until June 23rd.

After his time in Congress, he returned to the practice of law. Before his untimely death in life's prime, Hosmer had been made judge of the U.S. Maritime Court of Appeals.

It can be said of Titus Hosmer that he gave to his country much the same understanding, loyalty, and professional skills that he gave to his clients. Titus Hosmer earned not only the esteem of the Bar and the courts, but also the accolades of his state and his nation. A generous man above all, he became the patron of poet Joel Barlow, who under Hosmer's encouragement published the *Vision of Columbus*.

A Very Private Public Figure

SAMUEL HUNTINGTON

BIRTH: Scotland Society, Connecticut
July 5, 1731

DEATH: Norwich, Connecticut
January 5, 1796

COLONY: Connecticut

EDUCATION: Self-taught

PROFESSION: Lawyer

AT YORK TOWN: February 16, 1778–
May 31, 1778

At the age of eleven, as Samuel Huntington watched his older brother depart for college, he knew full well that no such glorious day would ever arrive for him. His father had decreed that, while Nathaniel was studying at Yale, Samuel would be learning how to make barrels as an apprentice to the local cooper. During his apprenticeship, however, Samuel had access to Greek and Latin literature in the library of his good friend and mentor, the Congregationalist minister Ebenezer Devotion. After completing his seven-year apprenticeship, he determined to study the law. Samuel borrowed the necessary books from two nearby lawyers, Jedediah Elderkin and Eliphalet Dyer, and set to work. By 1754, he was admitted to the Bar.

His next two decades were both prosperous and happy. As his law practice flourished, he moved to Norwich and purchased a home into which he moved his bride, Martha Devotion, daughter of his long-time friend. The Huntingtons, respectively described as "a wise and sedate man" and "a quiet, thrifty woman," managed a lively and serene household. Unable to have children, they reared a niece and a nephew as their own, cared for another boy until he reached college age, and filled their remaining rooms with young law students being trained by the head of the house.

Slowly but surely, Huntington's legal practice became a stepping-stone to politics. As a pillar of his church and the community, he gradually became the principal attorney for town affairs. His travels throughout the state as circuit judge brought him into contact with many leading figures in the political arena. As his prominence as a lawyer increased, he gained the reputation of being an excellent vote-getter, advancing from one local or state office to another.

As the storm clouds of revolution gathered, his retiring nature and habitual reticence prevented any public expression of his views. He took no part in the popular tavern discussions of the day, nor did he participate in demonstrations against British misrule. His role was never that of a leader but, rather, of an advisor to anti-British activists. Even if he had so desired, his lack of formal education would have prevented his making eloquent, impassioned speeches or writing inspirational articles. Even so, his ear was always attuned to the wishes of the people, and his legal decisions were a bulwark against oppression and tyranny.

It was, therefore, not surprising that when Connecticut elected delegates to replace Eliphalet Dyer and Silas Deane in Continental Congress, Huntington and Oliver Wolcott should be the chosen ones. Huntington had never been outside of Connecticut, nor had he ever seen anything like the "metropolis" of Philadelphia. He and Wolcott found lodgings at a boarding house on Third Street and took their seats in the historic Congress of 1776 on January 16th. While Wolcott attended the daily sessions, Huntington remained in their boarding house, stricken with smallpox.

He resumed his duties in February and suffered through the sweltering days of summer as the resolution for independence was under discussion. He had his instructions from Connecticut: "To consult, advise and resolve upon measures necessary for the defense, security and preservation of the rights and liberties of the said United Colonies." By July 2nd, he had interpreted that to mean total separation from the Mother Country, and so cast his ballot in the affirmative.

At York Town in 1778, where he again shared lodgings with Oliver Wolcott, his vote continued to reflect the wishes of his state and other New England Colonies. He was against price controls and the pension plan of half-pay for the lifetime of retired officers. He also worked hard for the ratification of the Articles of Confederation.

Probably the most arduous period of Huntington's public service career was from 1779 until 1781, when he served as the sixth President of Congress. The final ratification of the Articles of Confederation had transformed this position, formerly of little concern to the rest of the country, into the highest office in the land. Samuel Huntington found himself virtually the first President of the United States, responsible not to just one state but to thirteen. His change in title, from "Mister" to "Your Excellency," changed his whole way of life. President Huntington and First Lady Martha were soon installed in a Philadelphia mansion, where they were expected to receive and entertain foreign dignitaries as well as leaders of American society and politics—the extra expenses coming out of their own purse!

With no Vice President and little or no staff, this job demanded every ounce of dedication, patience, and prudence he could muster. The most onerous part of his Presidential routing was the voluminous correspondence. Letter writing was not his forte, but he performed his task to the best of his ability. His letters were formal, concise, matter of fact, and completely unbiased by personal opinion. His writing revealed nothing of the man behind the pen.

Huntington's crowning achievement was his election to the governorship of Connecticut in 1786, an office he held until his death in 1796. His funeral was as lavish and ostentatious as his lifestyle was private and simple. His body was laid to rest in a small cemetery near the Huntington home. In death, as in life, his heart was forever in Connecticut.

RICHARD LAW

BIRTH: Milford, Connecticut
March 7, 1733

DEATH: New London, Connecticut
January 26, 1806

COLONY: Connecticut

EDUCATION: Yale

PROFESSION: Lawyer

AT YORK TOWN: October 1, 1777–
December 6, 1777

That Richard Law would be a Connecticut Yankee in a court of law was practically ordained from the moment of his birth. One of seven children born to Jonathan Law and his fifth wife, Eunice (Hall) Andrew, he was named in honor of his great-grandfather, who emigrated from England and settled in Whethersfield in 1638. His father, a successful lawyer and Chief Judge of the Superior Court, was appointed Governor of the colony when Richard was only eight years old.

Governor Law was violently opposed to the religious reform movement known as the Great Awakening, and he prosecuted the enemies of the church as vigorously as those of the state. On one occasion, he ordered a clergyman to jail for preaching to the "sober dissenters" of Milford, and for a similar offense, he caused a visiting college president to be driven out of the colony as a vagrant. Under his father's tutelage, young Richard was reared in the strict tradition of his Puritan ancestors.

It was his mother, however, who influenced his choice of college. Eunice Law was the widow of Dr. Samuel Andrew, son of the Rector of Yale, and her nephew, Lyman Hall, a subsequent Signer of the Declaration of Independence, was already a student at that strongly Puritan institution. So, in due time, this son of a Harvard graduate was enrolled as a "son of Old Eli."

After his graduation from Yale in 1751, he read law with the famous American lawyer, poet, and historian Jared Ingersoll, and he was admitted to the Bar in 1755. Five years later, he married Ann Prentise, whose ancestors had come to America on the *Mayflower*.

Richard Law's transition from British subject to American patriot was made with little fuss or furor. He fully—but quietly—supported opposition to the Townshend Acts and to the Boston Port Bill, served on the Connecticut Council of Safety, and was one of two delegates chosen to confer with Washington on the defense of the colony in 1776. His reputation as a successful lawyer and faithful patriot made him a suitable delegate to the Continental Congress in 1774. Prevented from attending because of ill health, he was re-elected in 1776 only to be stricken by smallpox. This deprived him of the honor of signing the Declaration of Independence, a document that he fully endorsed and whose principles he had long advocated.

Richard Law did not take his seat in Congress until June 25, 1777, only three months before that body fled Philadelphia for the safety of York Town. During his entire career in Congress, which extended from 1780 through 1783, his exceptional capabilities as a jurist were never fully utilized. But at York Town he had the opportunity to use his talents in the final drafting of the Articles of Confederation, serving on a committee of three appointed to report any further articles that they should "judge proper to be added." Six of the seven they proposed were included in the completed version, which was adopted November 15, 1777.

Before leaving York Town in December, Law served on two other committees. One was directed "to inquire into the conduct of Colonel [George] Morgan, Agent of Indian Affairs," who was accused of "being unfriendly to the cause of America," a charge of which he was shortly cleared. The other, a prime example of congressional trivia, was appointed "to collect and digest the late useful discoveries for making molasses and spirits from the juice of cornstalks." If a report on this matter was ever forthcoming, it was not recorded in the *Journals of Congress*.

After the war, Law resumed his legal practice and took an active part in public life. He served as a County Court Judge and was a member of the State Supreme Court, where he was appointed Chief Justice. In 1789, with the establishment of the Federal Court system, his good friend, President Washington, appointed him the U.S. District Judge for his home state. His greatest legal contribution was the codification of the Statute Law of Connecticut, a task that he accomplished in co-operation with Roger Sherman, a long-time member of the Continental Congress.

In 1784, Judge Law was elected the first mayor of the newly charted city of New London, a position that he filled, together with his federal judgeship, until his death.

In name and in fact, he was a man of the Law, not only to the people of his native state but also to the early Americans of New England. Richard Law was born "a Connecticut Yankee," but he rightfully earned the title "Faithful Patriot."

ROGER SHERMAN

BIRTH: Newton, Massachusetts
    April 19, 1721

DEATH: New Haven, Connecticut
    July 23, 1793

COLONY: Connecticut

EDUCATION: County School, self-taught

PROFESSION: Shoemaker, lawyer, surveyor

AT YORK TOWN: April 25, 1778–
    June 27, 1778

Considering the number and variety of Roger Sherman's occupations and with their attendant responsibilities, there was little time or room in his life for foolishness. From the time he was nineteen years old, he bore the burden of supporting a family—first, his five younger brothers and sisters, and later, the fifteen children he fathered to two wives.

Robert was a little more than a baby when his family moved to a small farm in Stoughton, Connecticut. There, he attended country school under Samuel Dunbar, Pastor of the Congregational Church, from whom he acquired an unquenchable thirst for knowledge. It is said that while working at his cobbler's bench as an apprentice shoemaker, he usually had a book spread out before him. He was especially interested in the field of mathematics and lost no opportunity to pursue it.

His next move was to New Milford, Connecticut, where he and his older brother opened a successful general store; but he soon discovered that he could earn a larger income as a surveyor, an activity for which, through his study of mathematics, he was well prepared.

In 1750, he added a new venture to his growing list of enterprises. He began the publication of an almanac, which like Benjamin Franklin's *Poor Richard* contained astrological calculations, weather forecasts, advice to farmers, and aphorisms on all the Puritan virtues of honesty, hard work, thrift, piety, and plain living. Meanwhile, a friend had suggested that he study law, which he did and, as usual, strictly on his own. By 1754, he was licensed to practice in the courts of Litchfield County.

After the death of his wife, Elizabeth Hartwell, he and his seven children moved to New Haven, Connecticut, where he purchased two properties directly across the green from Yale. One was his residence; the other was a store stocked with provisions, books, and other goods aimed at the college trade. The shop soon became a gathering place for Yale tutors and students, ministers, and other townsmen of similar interests. There, they discussed books, current affairs, and enjoyed each other's intellectual companionship.

On a visit to his younger brother in Woburn, Massachusetts, he met and later married twenty-three-year-old Rebecca Prescott. Theirs was a happy marriage that produced eight additional children.

By the time American-British troubles reached a climax, Roger Sherman was a prosperous and highly respected public figure—shopkeeper, Deacon of the New Light Congregational Church, member of the Connecticut General Assembly, and Treasurer of Yale. He was, indeed, highly qualified to represent his state, along with Silas Deane and Eliphalet Dyer, at the First Continental Congress in 1774.

According to Dyer's account of their long journey to Philadelphia, they passed the time by "chatting, singing, discussing everything . . . scolding and making friends again every half hour." To what extent Sherman participated in such levity is unknown, but his Puritanism asserted itself on at least one occasion, much to the annoyance of Mr. Deane:

> He was against our sending our carriage over the Ferry this evening, because it is SUNDAY. So we shall have a scorching sun to drive forty miles in tomorrow!

In Congress, Sherman proved himself an able and dedicated delegate. Elected and re-elected for nine years, his attendance totaled 1,543 days. He was never an accomplished or polished speaker, a weakness he shared with his fellow delegate Eliphalet Dyer. In fact, the impatient John Adams said of them, "Dyer and Sherman speak often and long, but heavily and clumsily." However, after serving together on the committee of five to draft the Declaration of Independence, Adams pronounced Sherman "a Gift of Heaven; one of the most sensible men in the world, one of the soundest and strongest pillars of the Revolution."

During the post-war years and during the emergence of a new nation under a new constitution, Sherman continued to serve in a variety of roles. He made many friends—and just as many enemies. But he was always true to what, in his opinion, was in the best interests of the people. He had the honor of signing their three greatest charters—the Declaration of Independence, the Articles of Confederation, and the Constitution.

To describe him as a man "who never said a foolish thing" was, perhaps, a Jeffersonian exaggeration. And yet, it is uniquely applicable to a man who regarded public service "as a sacred trust . . . a direct calling from God Almighty."

A God-Fearing Patriot

WILLIAM WILLIAMS

BIRTH: Lebanon, Connecticut
    April 28, 1731

DEATH: Lebanon, Connecticut
    August 2, 1811

COLONY: Connecticut

EDUCATION: Harvard

PROFESSION: Merchant, Politician

AT YORK TOWN: September 30, 1777–
    December 3, 1777

Nowhere did religion have so much influence on politics as in Connecticut. The split in the Congregational Church—Old Lights and New Lights—determined a man's political party—conservative or liberal—and, thereby, also determined the results of elections. William Williams was the son and grandson of clergymen. His father, Solomon Williams, was a learned and popular pastor of Lebanon's New Light Congregation. Billy was reared in an atmosphere of Biblical and academic learning. After graduation from Harvard, he studied theology with his father, although he chose a different vocation, becoming a modestly successful shopkeeper. From an early age, his main interest was politics.

There was certainly no obstacle to Williams having a political career. Born and bred in Connecticut and a member of a respected religious family, this well-educated, successful young man could write his own ticket. He rose rapidly through the ranks of community offices—town clerk, treasurer, Selectman, and Justice of the Peace. After his marriage to Mary Trumbull, who was of equally impeccable background, he became head of his own strictly religious, church-going household, and he advanced to almost every position of authority offered by town, county, and state. His marriage was a happy one, and his letters never failed to express his love or his concern for his wife's health and welfare, as well as that of his three children.

By the time of the troubles with England, Williams was an influential man in both church and state affairs. He had no hesitation in aligning himself with the rebel cause. Convinced that he was in the right and firm in his faith that God was always on the side of good versus evil, he had no doubt of divine support, aid, and assistance. Williams had developed into an impassioned and eloquent public speaker as well as a forceful writer. His attacks against the King and Parliament were published in the *Connecticut Gazette*, and his speeches were well attended by patriotic audiences. Although he had some doubts that England would ever resort to the sword, he fearlessly advised his listeners, "Better to lose our blood than our liberties."

So successful were his efforts as Speaker of the lower House that Connecticut was psychologically ready for war even before the first shot was fired, and it was also highly receptive to the movement for independence. In 1776, Williams was elected to Congress. Unfortunately, he was not well suited for that service. His narrow, parochial views were a stumbling block to any leadership that he might have displayed.

William Williams had never been out of Connecticut before, except for a brief military excursion into New York during the French and Indian War. His trip to Philadelphia was "the most tiresome, sultry, and fatiguing journey" that he had ever experienced.

In his mind, only God and New Englanders were worthy of his trust . . . and not all of the latter. His relations with Eliphalet Dyer were strained, and he despised Silas Deane, who he thought was to blame for Philadelphia swarming with ambitious French officers awaiting promised promotions. His dislike of Frenchmen extended to a strong disapproval of French or any other foreign aid, preferring, instead, to rely on "the justice of the Cause and the infinite mercy of God."

He also disliked and distrusted New Yorkers and Southerners because of what he considered to be their anti-New England sentiments. As for Pennsylvanians:

> The people of this state appear to be, very many of them, weary of the stagnation of busi-

ness . . . whereby they have so much lost their Gain, which seems to be all the God they know, and are disaffected to the Cause . . . I had but a faint idea of the wickedness of the Country till I had traveled to this country, seen and heard so much of, and from the middle and southern parts. Well may we admire and adore the infinite Patience and long suffering of our God.

He had no more than set foot in Philadelphia ("the Mother of Harlots," as he described it) until he wanted to go home, a desire that was intensified by a severe attack of "the quick step"—military parlance for diarrhea. Nevertheless, he continued to represent his state until December 3rd, 1777. In York Town, he was able to see the completion of the Articles of Confederation and to rejoice over the victory at Saratoga, regarding which he wrote to Governor Trumbull:

> I doubt not Congress will appoint a Day of Thanksgiving on this great occasion, through out the Continent and may God give us heart to celebrate it in a right and acceptable manner.

He also had the personal satisfaction of the recall of Silas Deane from France and his replacement by John Adams, but his greatest satisfaction of all was that described in another letter to Trumbull:

> I have the sweet satisfaction of knowing I have served my country here with great Fidelity, and I hope, to some good purpose, and now the pleasing prospect of returning to my dear native Colony who have employed better Servants.

William Williams deserves to be remembered for more than his signature on the Declaration of Independence or for his service in Congress. He spared himself nothing in his work of recruiting, raising money, collecting supplies, and making unremitting efforts to protect and defend American freedom. His love and devotion to his country were second only to his love and reverence for his Creator. His unshakable faith was the single-most motivating force in the life of this Connecticut patriot.

A Man of Many Hats

OLIVER WOLCOTT

BIRTH: Windsor, Connecticut
    November 26, 1726

DEATH: Litchfield, Connecticut
    December 1, 1797

COLONY: Connecticut

EDUCATION: Yale

PROFESSION: Lawyer

AT YORK TOWN: February 16, 1778–
    June 27, 1778

Any reader of Oliver Wolcott's biography who is also familiar with children's literature cannot help but be reminded of Theodore Geisel's amusing tale, *The Five Hundred Hats of Bartholomew Cubbins*. Certainly, the hats worn by Wolcott did not equal those of Cubbins, but they were a large and varied assortment for one person. In addition to his schoolboy cap and his mortarboard from Yale, Wolcott wore the official "hats" of physician; Sheriff of Litchfield County; Captain, Colonel, and Major General of the Continental Army; Chief Justice of the Court of Common Pleas; Delegate to Congress; Signer of the Declaration of Independence; Lieutenant Governor; and Governor of Connecticut. Often, he wore two hats at the same time and sometimes had to do a quick-change act on the way from one assignment to the other.

Wolcott first attended Congress in 1775, but stricken by illness in June of 1776, he was forced to miss the day of official voting on independence in July—and also the day of the formal signing of the Declaration of Independence in August. However, upon his return in October, he affixed his signature to that important document. His activities on both the battle front and the political front demanded long periods of absence from home, during which his wife, Laura Collins Wolcott, with all the virtues of a Roman matron, saw to the education of their four children and conducted their domestic affairs, including the management of their small farm. Her one claim to fame as a participant in the Revolution was her achievement of making lead musket balls for the Continental Army. On July 9, 1776, a New York City mob, aroused by a public reading of the Declaration of Independence, had torn down a large equestrian statue of King George. The broken fragments were sent to Litchfield, where the women of the town turned them into much-needed ammunition. Laura Wolcott was credited with personally having made an impressive total of 4,250 rounds. Although her claim to historical importance may have been slight, her claim on Oliver Wolcott's attention and affection was limitless and undisputed.

Of the twenty-six letters written by Wolcott while at York Town, eleven were to his wife. From these letters evolves a concept of his devotion to his wife and family, his deep religious faith, a description of life in York Town, and a calendar of events. They also reveal something of his character and, to a degree, the sacrifices made necessary by service to his country.

Upon his arrival in York Town, which as a place he pronounced much more pleasant than Baltimore, Wolcott gave an account of his journey, which was less fatiguing than he had expected, and included the news that his horse had held out bravely and suffered nothing. "My separation from you," he wrote in April, "was always a most disagreeable circumstance to by being sent on publick business, and every repetition of an Appointment of this Nature becomes less agreeable." Later in the same letter:

> You take notice that in one of my letters I mentioned that I was well and enjoyed a flow of spirits. I hope you did not suppose I meant by it any Gayety of Temper. Your own experience, I believe will convince you that a flow of spirits in me is to be a little above dejection. As to the gloominess of the times which you mention, times, I admit, are bad, but I do not believe that God will consign this country to destruction. Light in time will arise and the happy days of Peace, fair, equitable and just peace will return. Suffer not your mind to be under any overwhelming solicitude on this account. God will take care of this people, and I trust that both you and I shall live to see the most convincing proofs of it in the establishment of their independency and safety.

Wolcott's faith in Providence and the outcome of the war were well justified, for he and Laura did enjoy the blessing of peace and the emergence of a new nation. Wolcott's personal contributions toward that peace were as many and varied as his "hats." As Commissioner of Indian Affairs, he attended the Conference of the Six Nations, gaining their temporary neutrality during the war. He also arbitrated land disputes between Pennsylvania, Connecticut, Vermont, and New York. He defended the Connecticut seacoast against British raids, and he participated in the New York Campaign of 1777, which culminated in the October surrender of Burgoyne at Saratoga. And it was the indomitable Laura whose patience, fortitude, intelligence, and devotion made possible the distinguished achievements of her husband.

The mortal remains of this husband-and-wife team of patriots are buried in the East Cemetery of Litchfield, a town where the name of WOLCOTT is visibly revered. The house that was their life-long residence was restored by one of their descendants in 1920 and is still standing. Although not open to the public, it is recognized as the oldest building in Litchfield's Historic District and is also listed as a National Historic Landmark, even as the family name of Wolcott appears today on the listing of great Americans.

$\mathcal{D}$ELAWARE

McKean, Thomas

$\mathcal{T}$HOMAS MCKEAN

BIRTH: Chester County, Pennsylvania
     March 19, 1734

DEATH: Philadelphia, Pennsylvania
     June 24, 1817

COLONY: Delaware

EDUCATION: Dr. Allison's Academy

PROFESSION: Lawyer

AT YORK TOWN: January 30, 1778–
          April 28, 1778
          May 11, 1778–
          May 31, 1778

Thomas McKean was born of Irish parents in Philadelphia, Pennsylvania, but was educated in Delaware. McKean was exposed to the political climate of both states throughout his lifetime, leaving both with honor and distinction. At the age of twenty, he was admitted to the Delaware Bar, but he soon extended his practice through New Jersey and Pennsylvania as well.

At twenty-nine, he married Mary Borden of Delaware. By 1765, he was already serving as Judge of the Court of Common Pleas and Orphan's Court in New Castle. As a member of the Stamp Act Congress, he registered his protest by making sure that no legal papers bore the hateful symbol of British tyranny—his court being the first in the colonies to defy the Crown by using unstamped paper.

In 1774, a year after the death of his first wife, he married Sarah Armitage of Philadelphia, where they began their new life together. In that same year, he was elected to the Continental Congress, which he served until peace was signed in 1783.

McKean was in a unique position. Although a resident of Pennsylvania, he represented the state of Delaware in Congress and was also Speaker of the House in the Delaware legislature. But in Congress during 1776, he put state matters aside to concentrate all his energies on the "All-for-one, one-for-all" issue of American independence. On July 1st, determined to break the deadlock between himself and his colleague, George Read, he sent an urgent message to Caesar Rodney, Delaware's third delegate, to come to the rescue. Already suffering from a terminal illness, Rodney rode all night through a severe thunderstorm, completing his eighty-mile journey just in time to cast his affirmative ballot—the decisive vote for the Declaration of Independence.

Meanwhile, McKean's revolutionary activities had not escaped the notice of the British, with the result that he and his family were exposed to their vengeance and persecution. As he wrote to his friend John Adams:

> I am hunted like a fox by the enemy, compelled to move my family five times in three months and at last fixed them in a little log house on the banks of the Susquehanna, but they were soon obliged to move again on account of the incursions of the Indians.

While Congress was at York Town, McKean was exposed not only to the pressures of that body but also to those exerted by his dual position as President of Delaware and Chief Justice of Pennsylvania. The war had not put a stop to civilian crime, and courts were still holding regular sessions. From time to time, he was forced to leave his seat in Congress to take his place on the bench as presiding judge. At one such session in Carlisle, a man was sentenced to death for burglary, and a woman found guilty of manslaughter was branded with an "M" on her left hand.

In his letters to his wife, McKean is revealed as a devoted husband and an affectionate, concerned father. No sooner did he hear of a grammar school being opened twenty-two miles from Lancaster than he enrolled two of his sons, Josey and Robert, and took a lively interest in their being outfitted properly for attendance. He wrote his wife:

> You must employ some taylor and seamstress without delay. As soon as you let me know that they are ready, I shall return home and take them to the school—the sooner the better.

McKean also tried to keep his wife informed about the current fortunes and misfortunes of the country at large and the business of Congress. In May of 1778, he was nothing short of ecstatic over the arrival of the Treaties with France:

> The Treaty between the United States of America and the MOST CHRISTIAN KING, proves that His Majesty of France is not only so, but also the most wise, most just, and most magnanimous Prince, not only in the world at present, but to be found in history.

Sarah McKean must have been more than a little dismayed on receipt of this letter, however, because her husband had been so carried away by its contents that he addressed it to Mary—his first, and long deceased, wife!

McKean's correspondence with his wife and colleagues reflects the events of history as well as those affecting his personal life. "I have lived to see the day when, instead of Americans licking the dust from the feet of a British Minister, the tables are turned," he wrote. "Acknowledge our independence or withdraw your fleets and armies, and we will treat with you for peace" was, as he told Sarah proudly, "agreed to unanimously, by thirty-one members, the whole number in York Town."

His interest in domestic affairs quickened with the approach of the adjournment to Philadelphia. On June 9th, he wrote to Sarah:

> I have tried to get you a maid, but in vain. I offered $20 a week, but the jades won't leave town. Do get one for the time we shall stay in Paxton. Let the price be what it may. In a very few days I expect Philadelphia will be evacuated by the enemy, and on the event, I must push there and take a house, while rents are low.

Although both Pennsylvania and Delaware claim Thomas McKean as their own, he lived the remainder of his life in Philadelphia and devoted himself to the service of the Commonwealth. He remained Chief Justice for twenty-two years and served three terms as Governor of Pennsylvania. His final resting place is in Philadelphia's historic Laurel Hill Cemetery. No clearer statement of this man's dedication and commitment to the ideals of his country is to be found than the following excerpt from a letter to Caesar Rodney: "I am determined never to give up the Independence of the United States, after so much expense of blood and treasure, whilst I have a breath to draw." His life is a testament to that vow.

GEORGIA

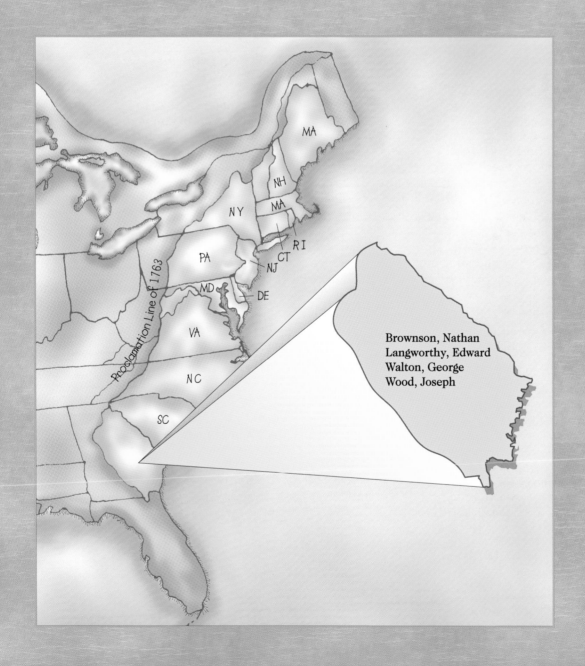

Brownson, Nathan
Langworthy, Edward
Walton, George
Wood, Joseph

Proclamation Line of 1763

A Physician of Public Trust

NATHAN BROWNSON

BIRTH: Woodbury, Connecticut
    May 14, 1742

DEATH: Liberty County, Georgia
    November 6, 1796

COLONY: Georgia

EDUCATION: Yale University

PROFESSION: Physician

AT YORK TOWN: September 30, 1777–
    October 9, 1777

Nathan Brownson was one of the twenty-five delegates present at the first business meeting of the Continental Congress assembled in York Town. Having completed his term as a delegate from Georgia, he departed on the ninth of October. His brief period of service in 1777, however, is by no means a measure of his contributions and overall value to the American Cause.

In 1774, shortly after establishing his residence and practice as a physician and smallpox inoculator in St. John's Parish, he became involved with men of his own political persuasion. A native of Connecticut, Brownson was pleased to discover that St. John's was a hotbed of patriotic sentiment. He joined the Whig public protests against the Stamp Act and became a member of the Second Provincial Congress, which met in Savannah July 4, 1775. He was a natural choice for the Continental Congress, and he was twice elected to that body. During the Revolutionary War, his medical education qualified him for the post of Surgeon General to a Georgia brigade.

Naturally, Brownson was greatly distressed by the British capture of Savannah late in 1778—and by their complete control of the state shortly thereafter. When he became Governor in 1781, after first having served as Speaker of the House, it became his personal responsibility to stabilize the state government, which was in a sorry state because of the flood of refugees who had fled to South Carolina to

23

escape the British occupation. During his four-and-a-half years as Governor, he worked for the return of these exiles and to quell the marauding bands of Tories who threatened to destroy what government there was.

His final contributions to the Revolution were made as Deputy Purveyor of Hospitals under General Nathaniel Greene, and after the war, this public-spirited man turned his attention to the educational and cultural welfare of his fellow citizens. He served as one of the trustees for the founding of the Georgia State University in 1784. He was also on the commission to erect new public buildings when the capital of Georgia was moved from Augusta to Louisville in 1785. Brownson was again elected to office as President of the State Senate between 1789 and 1791. He served as a member of the convention that framed Georgia's Constitution as well.

The more human side of Dr. Brownson is revealed by an anecdote related by a family friend, Major Andrew Maybank. The Major recalled that Brownson, jokingly, would sometimes warn his wife, Elizabeth McLean, that if she did not cater to his every whim, he would return after death to "plague" her. His widow, when pestered by a gnat, fly, mosquito, or any other insect, would sometimes accompany her futile swats with a fond smile of remembrance and the admonition "Go away, Dr. Brownson! Go away and stop bothering me!"

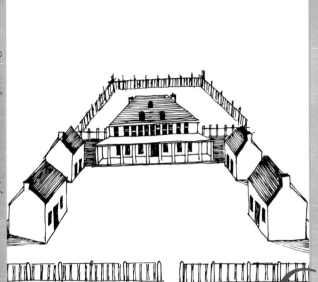

An Orphan from Georgia

EDWARD LANGWORTHY

BIRTH: Savannah, Georgia
1738

DEATH: Baltimore, Maryland
November 2, 1802

COLONY: Georgia

EDUCATION: Orphanage, Self-taught

PROFESSION: Teacher, Journalist

AT YORK TOWN: November 17, 1777–
June 27, 1778

Edward Langworthy's lot in life was never an easy one. With his parentage virtually unknown, he was reared and educated in Whitfield's Bethesda Orphan House. He enjoyed neither the creature comforts nor the academic advantages of the privileged Southern aristocracy, but he soon learned to make the most of what he had. Building on the schooling he received at the orphanage, he became a teacher there, and by the age of thirty-three, he was in charge of a school for "Academical Learning" established by that institution.

Langworthy's conversion from Loyalist to Revolutionist officially began in 1775, when he was chosen Secretary of the Committee of Safety. It culminated with his election to the Continental Congress in 1777.

He presented his credentials to Congress on November 17th and was immediately plunged into the maelstrom that threatened to engulf this intrepid band of patriots. According to a letter written on December 1st, his stay in York Town did not enjoy a happy start:

> The approach of General Howe towards Philadelphia obliged them [Congress] to adjourn to this most disagreeable Town, where everything is excessive, dear and scarce any accommodation to be procured. Since my arrival here, I have not been able to get private Lodgings, so that I am at present quite irregular as to the mode of living, which makes me very uneasy.

But his uneasiness must have subsided when he found quarters at Moore's Tavern, where he courted the Landlord's daughter, Mary, whom he married in July of 1778.

The records show Langworthy to have been faithful and efficient in the performance of his duties as a member of the Board of War, the Board of Treasury, and the Marine as well as various other committees. Except for two weeks in 1777 and approximately two months in 1778, he was the only delegate seated at the Georgia table.

Although never noted for originality or leadership, Langworthy was not without ideas of his own, nor did he lack the ingenuity and tenacity to turn them into reality—ergo, the Sago Powder Project. Shortly after his arrival in York, he sent a pound of sago powder to Dr. Benjamin Rush with a personal letter requesting the Philadelphia physician to assess its value to the sick and wounded and the possibility of using it in military hospitals. Sago, a food starch derived from the sago palm of Indonesia and Malaysia, was widely used in European hospitals, because it was easily digested and rich in carbohydrates. The sago promoted by Langworthy, however, was produced in Georgia by the widow of Samuel Bowen, who had developed it from the benne (sesame) plant that is native to this country. Receiving no reply from Dr. Rush, Langworthy next approached General Washington's paymaster, William Palfrey, on the subject. Eventually, he succeeded in obtaining an order for two tons of Bowen's sago powder for distribution to American military hospitals, together with the recommendation that "it should be used in every part of the Continent."

Despite this demonstration of a talent for salesmanship, Langworthy never pursued it as a career. Instead, his role during peace was that of a journalist and a teacher in the State of Maryland. He tried newspaper work for a time, served as a principal and teacher of Classics in the Baltimore Academy, and held a clerkship at the Custom's Office, but his real interest lay in the history of the country he had served so well. In 1792, he published the papers and biographical sketch of General Charles Lee and began a political history of his native state. Although the book was advertised in the *Georgia Gazette* for two dollars per copy, it never appeared in print. The manuscript was unfinished, lost, or destroyed. But one thing is certain, when he died in 1802, the book's completion was the only task undertaken by Edward Langworthy that he failed to bring to a successful conclusion.

A Carpenter's Apprentice

GEORGE WALTON

BIRTH: Farmville, Prince Edward County, Virginia (c. 1740/1750)

DEATH: Augusta, Georgia February 2, 1804

COLONY: Georgia

EDUCATION: Private, Self-taught

PROFESSION: Lawyer

AT YORK TOWN: September 1777– October 10, 1777

George Walton's life did not get off to an auspicious start. His mother and father both died before he reached school age, and he was placed in the care of his aunt and uncle, Martha and George Hughes Walton. When he reached adolescence, as was often the lot of sons from modest-income families, he was bound out as an apprentice. His master, Christopher Ford, was a carpenter and builder. Young Walton was more interested in building his primary schooling into a primary education, using books rather than a hammer and nails as his chosen tools. Mr. Ford, who believed reading to be synonymous with idleness, did not permit the boy to read during the day—and refused him candles at night. But the ambitious youth made his own lighting from pine knots, and he continued to pore over his books until his little torches burned out.

In 1769, George secured a release from his indenture and moved to Savannah, Georgia, where he began the study of law in the office of Henry Yonge. He proved an apt pupil and, after being admitted to the bar in 1774, a most successful lawyer.

As his law practice continued to grow, George Walton became more and more interested in, and concerned about, political affairs. Around the same time, he took an even livelier interest in romance and married Dorothy Camber. They became parents of two sons. He became secretary of the Provisional Congress in 1775 and also served as a member of the Committee of Intelligence. A member of the Council of Safety, as well, Walton later became its president.

At the beginning of the Revolutionary Period, Georgia's resistance to British in-roads on Colonial rights had taken the form of words rather than action. But by 1776, thanks to the patriotic efforts of men like Walton, Lyman Hall, Edward Langworthy, and Button Guinet, Georgia was ready to take up the cudgels for independence. George Walton took his seat in Congress on June 1st, 1776, in time to vote on the greatest of all issues. When he signed the Declaration of Independence at the age of twenty-six, he was the youngest member to do so.

When George Walton left the Continental Congress at York Town on October 10, 1777, he took up his previous home activities right where he had left off. In 1778, as a Colonel of the First Georgia Battalion, Walton participated in the defense of his state during the British siege of Savannah, where he was wounded and held prisoner for almost a year.

With the coming of peace, George Walton's career progressed even further. He served his state as Chief Justice and Justice of the State Superior Court, as Governor of Georgia, as a member of the state constitutional convention, and as a U.S. Senator in 1798 and 1799. His personal fortunes also increased to the point that he was able to build two homes—"Meadow Garden," on the northern edge of Augusta; and "College Hill," a country estate on Augusta's western outskirts. He also played a role in Indian affairs and in settling the boundary dispute between South Carolina and Georgia.

George Walton never lost his love of learning. He was a founder and trustee of Richmond Academy in Augusta and also of Franklin College (later the University of Georgia) in Athens. He was once again appointed a judge of Georgia's superior circuit in 1799, and he served in that capacity until his death five years later.

From humble beginnings to national acclaim, George Walton was one of the first to realize the American dream under the new constitutional government—a dream not only for himself, but also for the country for which he had sacrificed so much.

A Pennsylvania Transplant

JOSEPH WOOD

BIRTH: Pennsylvania
        1712

DEATH: Sunbury, Georgia
        September 1791

COLONY: Georgia

EDUCATION: Common School

PROFESSION: Planter

AT YORK TOWN: November 17, 1777–
        March 17, 1778

Unlike many present-day surgical transplants, there was no risk of rejection by the body politic of Georgia when Joseph Wood moved there from Pennsylvania. On the contrary, the Parish of St. Johns welcomed him with open arms as an ally in their support of the American cause. The people of St. John's Parish had loyally supported the Non-Importation Act and sought to form an alliance of trade and commerce with South Carolina, which had already acceded. Joseph Wood was enlisted as one of a committee of three to draft such a proposal to the General Committee of South Carolina. Although the Carolinians applauded the request, they refused to grant it on the grounds that it had come from only part of the province. Although Wood's first service to his adopted state was unsuccessful, he continued as a trusted and dependable public figure and was twice elected to the Continental Congress.

Presenting his credentials to Congress on the same day as his colleague Edward Langworthy, Wood arrived two days after the adoption of the Articles of Confederation, and he departed too soon to vote against Lord North's peace proposal. On December 27, 1777, however, he made his voice heard in the final disposition of York County Tory Daniel Batwell, the Anglican Rector of St. John's Church.

Joseph Wood's career also included military service with the Second Pennsylvania Regiment. He rose to the rank of Colonel and saw service in Canada. He was also appointed to the Marine Committee of the Continental Congress.

Following the war, he returned to his plantation of North New Port River in Liberty County, where he resided with his wife and four children for the remainder of his life. It would appear that his roots flourished as well in the red clay of Georgia as in the limestone soil of Pennsylvania. On his death in 1791, Georgia bestowed upon him every honor that would have been accorded a native son.

MARYLAND

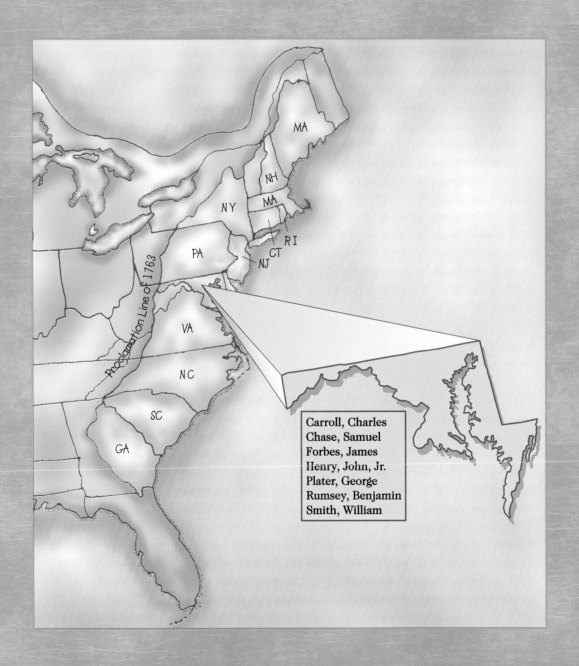

MA
NH
NY
MA
RI
PA
CT
NJ
VA
NC
SC
GA

Proclamation Line of 1763

Carroll, Charles
Chase, Samuel
Forbes, James
Henry, John, Jr.
Plater, George
Rumsey, Benjamin
Smith, William

CHARLES CARROLL OF CARROLLTON

BIRTH: Annapolis, Maryland
September 20, 1737

DEATH: Baltimore, Maryland
November 14, 1832

COLONY: Maryland

EDUCATION: European

PROFESSION: Gentleman of Property

AT YORK TOWN: September 30, 1777–
October 16, 1777
January 17, 1778–
June 27, 1778

Grandson of Charles Carroll the Settler and son of Charles Carroll of Annapolis, Charles Carroll of Carrollton lived a life of superlatives. He had the longest signature (twenty-six letters) and the longest lifespan (ninety-five years) of any gentleman in the Continental Congress. He was the wealthiest man in the colonies, the largest landowner, the first and most influential Catholic statesman, and because he outlived all the others, the most venerated signer of the Declaration of Independence.

Barred from voting, holding office, or practicing law because of his religion, the young Carroll, on completing his extensive European education, took no part in politics. He enjoyed the life of an aristocratic country gentleman, managing the family estate and building Carrollton Manor on a ten-thousand-acre tract deeded him by his father in 1765. After his marriage to his seventeen-year-old cousin, Mary (Molly) Darnall, the young couple divided their time between the social life of Annapolis and the domesticity of Doughoregan Manor, the Carroll ancestral home in Howard County.

But in 1773, he became personally and politically incensed by Governor Eden's high-handed imposition of increased government service fees on an already economically depressed people. Writing under the sobriquet "FIRST CITIZEN" in a series of newspaper debates with Daniel Dulaney, the Governor's advocate, Carroll won such public acclaim that he suddenly emerged as part of a new political faction destined to lead his province to independence and statehood.

"First Citizen" Carroll would have been the popular choice as delegate to the Continental Congress in 1774, but as a Catholic, he was ineligible. The official delegation so valued his opinion, however, that he was invited to attend as an observer, and in 1776, he was appointed to the commission that unsuccessfully attempted to form an alliance with Canada.

Although not elected to Congress until July 4th, 1776, Carroll had used his influence with the reluctant Maryland Assembly to rescind their anti-independence instructions, and on August 2nd, 1776, he affixed his signature to the Declaration of Independence.

The *Journals of Congress* record Carroll's presence at York Town during the early October debates on the Articles of Confederation, and although he returned to the Maryland Assembly before the Articles were finally adopted, he had previously expressed the opinion that "[a] Confederacy formed on a rational plan will certainly add much weight and consequence to the United States collectively and give great security to each individually."

Carroll resumed his seat in January and was almost immediately ordered to Valley Forge as a member of a committee to reform the army's organization, economy, and discipline. Against the background of a Congress divided into Pro-Gates and Pro-Washington factions by the Conway Cabal, this was a critical assignment. That his loyalty to Washington prevailed is attested to by an indignant statement from Thomas Conway himself; "He [Carroll] told me a few days ago almost literally that any body that displeased or did not admire the Commander in Chief ought not to be kept in the army."

To a man of Carroll's cultivated mind and business acumen, the petty bickering that frequently delayed congressional action sometimes proved irksome. "The Congress do worse than ever," he complained to Governor Johnson in the spring of 1778. "We murder time and chat it away in idle, impertinent talk." Nevertheless, on June 27th, the day of adjournment to Philadelphia, Carroll had good reason to applaud the action of Congress at York Town "for signing the treaties with France, and in unanimously rejecting any and all British negotiations for peace which did not specifically recognize American independence."

Charles Carroll lived to enjoy the liberty that he helped establish for his church, his state, and his nation. He lived to see Roman Catholics regale the civil rights of which they had been deprived since 1718. He lived to see the adoption of the U.S. Constitution, to serve as state senator, and to represent his native Maryland in the first Federal Congress from 1789 to 1792. He lived to see the dawn of the 19th century and to share in its progress and prosperity. He also served as a director of the Chesapeake and Ohio Canal Company, the First and Second Banks of the United States, and the Baltimore and Ohio Railroad, for which he laid the cornerstone in 1828.

His body was entombed in the private chapel on the family estate at Doughoregan Manor, a fitting resting place for the grandson of that first Charles Carroll, who came to America with the dream and the motto: "Anywhere so long as there be freedom." By his action in securing that freedom, Charles Carroll of Carrollton earned his place in history not only as "First Citizen" but as a superlative patriot.

The Stormy Petrel

SAMUEL CHASE

BIRTH: Somerset County, Maryland
April 17, 1741

DEATH: Washington, D.C.
June 19, 1811

COLONY: Maryland

EDUCATION: Private tutor, Law firm of
Hammond and Hall

PROFESSION: Lawyer, Businessman

AT YORK TOWN: October 1, 1771–
October 18, 1777
March 23, 1778–
June 27, 1778

Seldom has any public figure in American history been showered with as many epithets as Samuel Chase. A man of action—but not of few words—his flights of oratory labeled him "[t]he Demosthenes of Maryland." To his admirers and fellow patriots, he was "[t]he Torch that lighted up the revolutionary flame in Maryland." To his Tory enemies, he was "a busy, restless incendiary"; "a ringleader of mobs"; and "an inflammatory son of Discord." To his colleagues in Congress and members of the Bar, he was "Bacon Face!"

In less troubled times, he might have enjoyed a quiet, comfortable life in the profession for which his studies in the prestigious Annapolis law firm of Hammond and Hall had prepared him. By the time he was twenty-two years old, his career was well launched. He was a member of the Maryland Assembly, had been admitted to the Bar, and with his bride, the former Anne Baldwin, had set up his own establishment in Annapolis, where he was recognized as one of the most promising young advocates of the Province. But the political events of 1764 and 1765 unleashed in him a fury of protest that catapulted him into leadership of the patriotic resistance, a position for which he was physically and intellectually suited. His big, burly frame, his booming voice, incisive mind, and his persuasive oratory made him a force to be reckoned with, whether as a member of the riotous Sons of Liberty or the more circumspect Committee of Correspondence.

When the first Continental Congress met in Philadelphia, Samuel Chase was there. When in 1776 a commission was sent to Montreal to win over Canada, Chase was a member. When he returned from that unsuccessful mission in June to find a motion for independence before the House, he rushed back to Annapolis in a whirlwind campaign to gain Maryland's support.

His personal conviction was that "by the God in heaven [I] owe no allegiance to the King of Great Britain." This fervor was not reflected in the Maryland Convention, however, which was still worded to favor reconciliation, but Chase took the issue directly to the people. County by county, he rolled up a majority for Richard Henry Lee's resolution. Shortly before the deadline, he wrote to John Adams:

> Fryday Evening at 9 o'clock: I am this Moment from the House to procure an Express to follow the Post with an Unan Vote of the Convention for Independence . . . see the glorious effects of County Instructions . . . our people have fire if not smothered.

Riding 150 miles as quickly as he could, he reached Philadelphia in time for Maryland's vote to be cast in favor of the Declaration.

Chase was quick to recognize the urgency of forming a confederacy. Without it, he wrote in 1776:

> [W]e shall remain weak, distracted and divided in our councils: our strength will decrease: we shall be open to all the arts of the insidious Court of Britain, and no foreign Court will attend to our applications for assistance.

Article by article, amendment by amendment, he debated the conflicting issues of the Articles of Confederation, convinced that all "might be settled if candour, justice and the real interests of America were attended to."

From 1796 until 1811, Samuel Chase enjoyed the most fruitful period of his career as Associate Justice of the U.S. Supreme Court. His knowledge of the law, his grasp of political science, and the forceful expression of his far-reaching opinions ranked his performance second only to that of Chief Justice John Marshall. But even on the Supreme Bench, his turbulent disposition led to charges of political partisanship, judicial improprieties, and an impeachment trial. Despite twenty-five of the thirty-four members of the Senate belonging to the opposing political party, the impeachment failed. Once again, "The Petrel" had weathered the storm.

Since the time that the body of Judge Chase was laid to rest in Old St. Paul's churchyard in Baltimore, there have been many evaluations of his life and character. Perhaps the most accurate is to be found in his own work. Although removed from their original time and context, they may well be the key to the conflict and complexity of the dynamic man who signed himself Samuel Chase:

> I am really diffident of myself, I shall endeavor to act my part well. My Soul has been chagrined at certain Conduct, but I love my country.

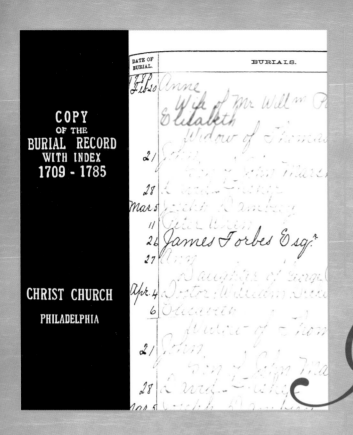

COPY OF THE BURIAL RECORD WITH INDEX 1709 - 1785

CHRIST CHURCH PHILADELPHIA

JAMES FORBES

BIRTH: Charles County, Maryland
     1731

DEATH: Philadelphia, Pennsylvania
     March 25, 1780

COLONY: Maryland

EDUCATION: Common School

PROFESSION: Merchant

AT YORK TOWN: February 1778–
     April 18, 1778

James Forbes was the son of Scotsman John Forbes, who married a widow with five children, so the boy grew up with two stepbrothers and three stepsisters. Reared in a family of modest means, young Forbes did not have any special educational advantages. In 1757, however, he went into partnership with George Maxwell, and within five years, he had become a successful businessman. His success and influences certainly increased as well, for he was appointed a State Court judge in 1770. He was also sufficiently known and respected throughout his homeland to be elected Justice of the Peace and Tax Commissioner. He later became a representative in Maryland's Lower House.

Forbes' call to the Continental Congress came three days before Christmas of 1777, but he did not attend until January. He was re-elected in November of 1778 and again in December of 1779. During the two months he served at York Town, he was a member of the Committee of Commerce together with Francis Lewis and William Ellery.

At the time of his death in 1780, James Forbes was still a member of Congress, which by then had returned once more to Philadelphia. The estate of this little-known character who rose from modest means consisted of two lots in Charles County and a quite substantial estate in St. Mary's County. He, along with countless other patriots about whom we know little, died in the service of this country. He is buried with many other, better-known patriots of his day in the graveyard of Christ Church in Philadelphia.

JOHN HENRY
LAWYER, STATESMAN, GOVERNOR

BORN IN DORCHESTER Co. 1750
DIED 1798

CONT'L CONGRESS 1777-1788
U.S. SENATE 1789-1797
GOVERNOR of MARYLAND 1797-1798

HONORED FOR HIS WISDOM
AND
POLITICAL INTEGRITY

Arch Enemy of Profiteers

JOHN HENRY, JR.

BIRTH: Dorchester County, Maryland
November, 1750

DEATH: Dorchester County, Maryland
December 16, 1798

COLONY: Maryland

EDUCATION: College of New Jersey
(Princeton)
Middle Temple, London

PROFESSION: Lawyer

AT YORK TOWN: February 1778 –
May 1778

John Henry, Jr., was born into a Maryland family of substance and prominence. His father, Colonel John Henry, was an important figure as a representative of Dorchester County in the provincial Assembly. John Henry, Jr., received an excellent education, first at the West Nottingham Academy in Cecil County and then at Princeton. While a law student in London, he became only too well versed in British policies toward America. He returned home strongly convinced of the need for change. In 1775 he began practicing law in Dorchester County and was elected as a member of the Maryland General Assembly.

His outspoken antagonism toward British restrictions on colonial liberties, coupled with his personal abilities, made him an ideal choice for the Continental Congress, where he served from 1778 to 1781 and again from 1784 until 1787. During his years in Congress, especially while he was at York Town, Henry was outraged by the citizens who made huge profits at the expense of their country. In his first letter written at York Town, which was dated February 14, 1778, he complained to Governor Johnson:

> The state of our army is critical. Four months pay, if not more, are due them, and no money in the Treasury to satisfy their just and reasonable Demands. The Press is hard work, and attended with all vigilance and care, and has been for some time past; near a Million a week is now

made, and yet our demands are greater than we can answer. They come in from all parts of the Continent. The avarice of our people and the extravagant prices of all commodities, joined with the imperfect management of our affairs, would expend the monies of Chile and Peru.

For the want of pay, of clothes, and provisions, our army is decreasing every hour. Not by one or two at a time, but from seven to twelve. By a letter from Colonel Smith, he tells me some of the troops have been eight days at different times, without meat and only a bare allowance of flour.

Later, to Nicholas Thomas, Speaker of the Maryland House of Delegates, he wrote:

The wants and distress of our army no doubt has reached your ears. To recapitulate them would give you unnecessary pain as it is out of your power to afford any relief. They have received a short, temporary supply. How long it will continue, I do not certainly know, but I have every reason to believe but a few weeks. The causes which have produced these Evils, I trust will be a subject of serious inquiry. It is highly necessary they should, if no other views were to be answered by it, than the prevention if such mischiefs in future. Where men are virtuous and active, and properly supplied with money, it appears to me unaccountably strange in a country like this, the very lap of plenty, that an army like ours should be on the very brink of destruction for the want of common necessaries. And what is beyond measure astonishing, many of the soldiers for the want of a little straw to lie upon, are daily dropping into the grave. I wish for better times, and I am sure we have a right to expect better men and management. Many of the officers in the great civil department I am convinced are highly criminal, and I expect they will be found so.

Henry's patriotic services were recognized and honored in his native state. He and Charles Carroll were the first senators elected to the United States Senate, and he was elected the ninth Governor of Maryland on November 13, 1797. After his first term, he declined to run for a second because of ill health. Five weeks later, he died at the Henry ancestral estate in Dorchester County. His descendants erected a monument in his honor in the Protestant Episcopal churchyard in Cambridge Maryland, but no monument is needed to remind present-day Americans to revere the memory of this high-principled patriot who placed the interests of his country above those of himself.

Like Father–Like Son

GEORGE PLATER

BIRTH: St. Mary's County, Maryland
November 8, 1735

DEATH: Annapolis, Maryland
February 10, 1792

COLONY: Maryland

EDUCATION: William and Mary College

PROFESSION: Lawyer

AT YORK TOWN: April 18, 1778–
June 27, 1778

George Plater, born on the family estate of Sotterly, near Leonardtown, Maryland, was the grandson of the first George Plater, who emigrated from England and became a man of local influence and importance. He was also the son of the second George Plater, who took an active part in the provincial government. In turn, he was father of Thomas Plater, who followed the Plater pattern by attending William and Mary College, becoming a lawyer, and serving as a representative in the 7th and 8th Congresses of the United States.

In 1760, while on a visit to England, Plater became acquainted with the last Lord Baltimore, who was so impressed with the young man that he recommended him to the Proprietary Governor of Maryland. From 1767 to 1773, he served as a naval officer of the Patuxent District, the same position previously held by both his father and his grandfather.

Despite being the King's Man in the provincial government, he was sympathetic to the rights of his fellow citizens and supportive of colonial opposition to British oppression. He did not display any real leadership in the opposition movement, however, until 1776. In February of that momentous year, he was appointed by the Council of Safety to be one of three collectors of gold and silver to pay for military operations against Canada, and he also co-operated with the Virginia Commissioners in erecting beacons along both sides of the Potomac.

41

In May, he became a Council of Safety member himself, and by September, he was involved in drafting legislation to form a new state government.

George Plater was married twice. His first wife, Hannah Lee, died within ten months of their marriage. His second, Elizabeth Rousby, was the mother of Thomas Plater and five other children. According to John Bannister, a delegate from Virginia who became acquainted with the couple during their mutual stay in York Town, the Platers were most agreeable company and a welcome addition to his social life.

Plater's participation in public life took place during times when his services were most needed. He came to the Continental Congress when attendance was at a minimum. While at York Town, only two others were present to represent the state of Maryland—John Henry and Charles Carroll of Carrollton—in addition to himself. He presided over the Maryland Convention for the ratification of the U.S. Constitution when that body was in a state of discord, and he conducted himself in such a manner as to be awarded a vote of thanks from each of the disagreeing factions. He also served as one of the electors who voted for Washington as the first President of the United States. When Plater was elected the sixth Governor of Maryland in November, 1791, it was then that negotiations for the location of the new nation's Capital to be in Maryland were completed.

While George Plater did not make any overtly significant contributions to the Revolution, he remains a fine example of a patriotic American for whom concept of public service, from generation to generation, embraced the community, state, and nation.

BENJAMIN RUMSEY

BIRTH: Cecil County, Maryland
October 6, 1734

DEATH: Joppa, Harford County, Maryland
March 7, 1808

COLONY: Maryland

EDUCATION: College of New Jersey
(Princeton)

PROFESSION: Planter, Lawyer

AT YORK TOWN: November 1777–
December 24, 1777

Benjamin Rumsey was the third son of William Rumsey, who died when the boy was about eight years old. Benjamin was reared by his mother, Sabina Blaidenburgh, and a stepfather, Nathaniel Rigbie. He was raised in the Anglican church and, on reaching his majority, became a planter in addition to his practice of law, where he served the courts of Baltimore, Cecil, and Howard Counties. In 1774, he became a representative in the Lower House for Cecil County.

During the Revolution, Rumsey was a member of the Maryland Convention in 1775 and served on the committee to prepare instructions for state delegates to the Continental Congress. The following year, he became a member of the Council of Safety, and he was also appointed Colonel of the Lower Battalion of Harford County's militia.

Rumsey reported to Congress at York Town early in November of 1777 to relieve Samuel Chase, who was eagerly awaiting his arrival. During his brief term of service, Rumsey interested himself in the promotion of Maryland officers. On November 4th, he was able to inform Benedict Edward Hall, Justice of Harford County, that William Smallwood had been elevated to the rank of Brigadier, the only Marylander to receive such a promotion until 1779. Of Smallwood, Rumsey wrote that his promotion was based on the quality of leadership displayed during his training of the first Maryland troops.

They were, Rumsey said, "well trained, well officered, well clothed, cut a fine figure, and did remarkable service."

Following his Congressional service, Rumsey was appointed a General Court judge, but he declined that honor. However, the following year he became the chief judge of Maryland's Court of Appeals and held that position until his death in 1806.

At his life's end, Benjamin Rumsey's holdings were assessed at more than eighteen-thousand dollars (including slaves and properties). But an assessment of his life and character as an American patriot transcends all monetary value.

William the First

WILLIAM SMITH

BIRTH: Lancaster County, Pennsylvania
April 12, 1728

DEATH: Baltimore County, Maryland
March 27, 1814

COLONY: Maryland

EDUCATION: Common School

PROFESSION: Mercantile Enterprises

AT YORK TOWN: October 4, 1777–
December 24, 1777

Between 1774 and 1927, there were fourteen members of Congress named William Smith! The first of these distinguished men, Williams was a delegate from Maryland elected February 15, 1777. This colonial William Smith moved from Donegal Township in Lancaster County, Pennsylvania, to Baltimore, Maryland, on May 1, 1761. He lived in Baltimore the rest of his life, and he began to serve his new home state in 1774 as a member of the Committee of Correspondence. The following year, he became part of the Committee of Observation. In 1777, with his Congressional duties, he also served as an appointed member of the Naval Board.

The fifty days spent at York Town in 1777 were busy ones for William Smith. He labored over the Articles of Confederation, rejoiced over the great news from Saratoga, attended the Thanksgiving Service, and worried with the rest of Congress over the dangers in the terms of Burgoyne's surrender to General Gates. There was also a foreign affairs matter of deep concern that affected him as a member of the Committee of Commerce. Thomas Morris, the illegitimate half-brother of Robert Morris, had been appointed Superintending Agent to the Commercial Business of the United States in France. The young man had come well recommended by his brother Robert, who had also provided him with a good education and experience in his own counting house. However, Thomas proved unworthy of his brother's trust or his country's welfare. When the news of his misconduct reached Robert Morris and the Congress, orders for his immediate dismissal were signed and sealed by the Committee of Congress. William Smith was an active and conscientious member of this group.

This first William also served as a member of Congress from March 4, 1778, to March 3, 1791. He became the first Auditor of the U.S. Treasury, and he served in this capacity from July 16, 1791, to November 27, 1791, by which time he had come to be a Federalist.

The credentials and career of William Smith, the first of the long succession of Congressmen by that name, justified the honor he enjoyed by serving Congress at York Town.

MASSACHUSETTS

Proclamation Line of 1763

NH
NY
PA
CT
NJ
MD
DE
VA
NC
SC
GA

Adams, John
Adams, Samuel
Dana, Francis
Gerry, Elbridge
Hancock, John
Holten, Samuel
Lovell, James

Defiant Defender

JOHN ADAMS

BIRTH: Braintree, Massachusetts
October 30, 1735

DEATH: Quincy, Massachusetts
July 4, 1826

COLONY: Massachusetts

EDUCATION: Harvard College

PROFESSION: Lawyer

AT YORK TOWN: September 30, 1777–
November 8, 1777

John Adams not only defied his King and Mother Country in the defense of Liberty, but he also defied his co-patriots when he defended the perpetrators of the Boston Massacre in the protection of Justice. Self-styled as "puffy, vain, [and] conceited," this brilliant statesman from Massachusetts had a stubborn strength of character surpassed by none of the other Founding Fathers.

John Adams came to York Town with the rest of the Continental Congress, forced to leave Philadelphia by the advance of General Howe in September of 1777. To these men, each with a price on his head, the three sevens within that year's date bore a striking resemblance to a row of gallows. John Adams knew only too well that the price on his own head would be an amount the enemy would gladly pay should 1777 indeed become, as the Tories prophesied, "The Year of the Hangman."

More fortunate than most delegates, Adams found comfortable lodgings at the home of General Daniel Roberdeau, a Pennsylvania delegate who had opened his comfortable home to his fellow congressmen.

During his brief stay in York Town, the most pressing matter before Congress was the completion of the Articles of Confederation, a task that required infinite patience and seemingly endless debate. Although in total agreement with the need for union, Adams frequently defied the entire

Congress—as well as delegates from his home state—in defending his own points of view.

The three main issues dividing Congress during their debates on the Articles were the manner of voting, the apportionment of expenses, and the power of Congress to "settle the claims of the South Seas," which meant the fixing of Western boundaries. Small wonder that John Adams likened the settlement of these differences to the difficulty of making "thirteen clocks strike together." Nevertheless, through discussion, compromise, and sheer exhaustion, by November 15th (still observed in York, Pennsylvania, as ARTICLES OF CONFEDERATION DAY), the Articles were completed.

John Adams left York before what he termed "the rope of sand" was actually adopted. On November 7th, he was granted a leave of absence to visit his family, and the next day, having expressed the fear he would not recognize his own children were he to be absent much longer, he left for Boston. Who could have guessed, as he mounted "his little pony" in front of the Roberdeau house, that his next visit to York would be as the second President of the United States of America?

Meanwhile, before he even reached his home, Congress had elected him Commissioner to the Court of France. Excerpts from a letter to Roberdeau from a devoted Abigail Adams describe her reactions to the news:

> The distinction given him by his country must be at the expense of my present tranquillity and happiness . . . Danger and hazard, fear and anxiety will ever be uppermost in my mind . . . I shall endeavor as much as possible to leave him free to act as he thinks best.

The complete career of John Adams—Jurist, Legislator, Ambassador to France and England, Vice President and President of the United States, and lifetime Defender of American Liberty and Independence—has been recounted in volume after volume. His life ended at the age of ninety-one, on July 4th, 1826, the fiftieth anniversary of the signing of the Declaration of Independence. By a strange coincidence of history, the author of the immortal document, Thomas Jefferson, his beloved adversary, died on the same day. Adams' final words were "Jefferson still lives" . . . but Jefferson had preceded his "cantankerous friend" by a few hours.

But, so long as there are men and women who believe that revolution is a continuing process, that there is always liberty to be won and chains to be broken, John Adams and Thomas Jefferson will still be very much alive.

The Great Agitator

SAMUEL ADAMS

BIRTH: Boston, Massachusetts
September 27, 1722

DEATH: Boston, Massachusetts
October 2, 1803

COLONY: Massachusetts

EDUCATION: Boston Latin School, Harvard

PROFESSION: Propagandist

AT YORK TOWN: September 30, 1777–
November 8, 1777
June 27, 1778

In 1777, the greatest prize for any Tory hangman would have been Samuel Adams, because more than any other individual, he had inflamed the colonies to resistance against British aggression and to a war for complete independence.

A London newspaper boast that the heads of Adams and John Hancock would soon be exposed on Temple Bar was unfulfilled, and plans to arrest that patriotic pair were foiled by a warning from Paul Revere on what Adams called the "Glorious Morning" of April 19, 1775.

The British had ample reason for attempting to silence this gifted and dedicated "rabble rouser." From the passage of the Stamp Act in 1764 until his death in 1802, Adams never ceased to exhort the "timid and over-prudent" to take strong action against any form of tyranny of temporizing policy.

His prolific and seditious writings enraged the King and fired local resentment of British troops, thereby leading to the Boston Massacre. With the tax on tea, the spark of rebellion was rekindled by Samuel Adams, who incited and participated in the Boston Tea Party.

His greatest threat to Britain was his rousing of support for Boston from other colonies less affected by oppression from the Crown. He was the acknowledged leader of the gradual shift in public opinion from resistance to independence as the only remedy for the evils of the time.

Both Samuel Adams and his second cousin, John Adams, served as delegates to the First and Second Continental Congress. Both proudly—and almost gleefully—signed the Declaration of Independence. Samuel, however, attended those immortal sessions attired in a wardrobe assembled and donated by neighbors who could not bear to see their representative in his usual shabby dress. Although born the son of a wealthy brewer and educated for the law, Adams had skipped from job to job (none of them successful), and after his father's death, he managed to lose the entire family fortune. Obviously, he would never be a financial success, and he did not seem to care. Even when he was unable to support his family, he spoke of his poverty as "his pride."

Samuel Adams was one of the first congressmen to arrive in York Town. Although his stay was brief, it was long enough for him to see the completion of the Articles of Confederation, for him to rejoice over the victory at Saratoga, and for him to serve on almost every important committee.

Congress lost two of its greatest leaders when both Adams delegates were granted leaves of absence on the same day. It is safe to say that no man did more toward bringing about the Revolution and effecting the independence of the colonies than Samuel Adams. Without the "Great Agitator," who lies in Boston's Old Granary Burial Ground, the history of the United States might well have taken a very different turn.

Delegate/Diplomat

FRANCIS DANA

BIRTH: Charlestown, Massachusetts
June 13, 1743

DEATH: Cambridge, Massachusetts
April 25, 1811

COLONY: Massachusetts

EDUCATION: Harvard

PROFESSION: Lawyer

AT YORK TOWN: January 1778–
May 31, 1778

While in Paris, John Adams received a letter from his wife, Abigail, asking him to send her "a blue and white silk quilt like the one Mr. Dana sent his wife." It was only natural for these two Massachusetts families to be friends. In fact, the lives of John Adams and Francis Dana paralleled each other in many ways. Both were graduates of Harvard, both practiced law in Boston, often working together on the same case. Both served in the Continental Congress, both were in the diplomatic service, and both were patriots of the first order. Although Adams was eight years Dana's senior and, unlike the latter, had not been born to wealth and position, the two men had much in common.

When the port of Boston was closed by order of Parliament in 1775, Dana went to England armed with letters from influential Americans aimed at convincing the British to reconsider. Upon his return from this unsuccessful mission, he reported to George Washington that no cessation of hostilities was to be expected. He was elected to Congress in the fall of 1776 and again at the beginning of 1778.

Francis Dana served only a brief time in York Town, because he was sent as Chairman of the Committee on Army Reorganization to Valley Forge, where he remained until May 31st of that year. Like his fellow committee workers, he was horrified by conditions at the camp. On February 16, 1778, he wrote to Elbridge Gerry describing threats of desertion by two regiments, which had since been calmed by the prudence of their officers. He continued:

> But no prudence or management, without meat, can satisfy the hungry men. In plain terms, 'tis probable this army will disperse if the Commissary Department is so damnably managed. Good God! how absurd to attempt an expedition into Canada when you cannot feed this reduced army!

Francis Dana also served with Gouverneur Morris and William Drayton on the Congressional committee to which Lord North's conciliation proposals were submitted and unanimously rejected. The most exciting, frustrating, and adventurous period of Dana's life began in November, when he sailed with John Adams for Paris as Secretary of the Legation to negotiate peace terms with Britain. The party of five—Adams, his two sons (thirteen-year-old John Quincy and eleven-year-old Charles), John Thatcher (his personal secretary), and Dana—set sail on the French frigate *La Sensible*, November 13, 1779. It did not reach Paris until February 9, 1780, because *La Sensible* did not live up to her name. The voyage was rough, everyone was seasick, and a dangerous leak forced a landing at Ferrol, Spain. This necessitated the party to undertake a thousand-mile trek across the Pyrenees, through Spain, into France. The resourceful Adams engaged two coaches stocked with provisions and a handsome, four-volume Spanish Dictionary, but nevertheless, the trip was a nightmare. Even the seasoned traveler, Mr. Adams, considered it the worst of his life.

In France, Dana and Adams ran into more trouble, this time with the French ministers who insisted that the welfare of France be considered in any and all peace negotiations. The two men then left France for Holland, where they were successful in obtaining a sizable loan for America. Upon their return to Paris, Dana received word from Congress that he had been appointed as minister plenipotentiary to the Russian Court. He was ill equipped for the job. He spoke no foreign language, had no experience in making foreign travel arrangements, nor had he first-hand knowledge of the skill and finesse demanded in diplomacy. Furthermore, Congress had not allocated any money for an interpreter or secretary. Fortunately, he was able to persuade his old friend, Adams, to lend him John Quincy, who was fluent in French and able to do secretarial work as well. Adams also advanced the money for his son's travel expenses and supplied plenty of free advice and encouragement. Dana should "be candid as to his position on all issues and seek the advice of experienced diplomats." "And," he added, "The United States of America have nothing dishonorable to propose to any court of all nations . . . her cause is that of all nations and all men, and it needs nothing but to be explained to be approved."

Dana's two years in Russia were occupied in vain attempts to do the necessary explaining. Catherine the Great refused to receive him or to acknowledge the United States as a new and independent nation. However, when he finally departed for home in 1783, he had managed to talk with several high-ranking Russians. As Adams had told him at the beginning of his mission, "If without being received, we can gain and communicate information, we shall answer a good end."

In later years, Dana served as Chief Justice of Massachusetts, vigorously supported the new Constitution, and worked hard for its ratification. He was also interested in the arts and sciences as well as in the literary life of Boston. Francis Dana is remembered as being a typical member of the New England aristocracy, having a high sense of honor and of public duty and the conviction that birth and station determined the guardians of the people. He was an eloquent spokesman for independence, the Federalist party, and the rights of freemen as guaranteed by law.

ELBRIDGE GERRY

BIRTH: Marblehead, Massachusetts
July 17, 1744

DEATH: Washington, D.C.
November 23, 1814

COLONY: Massachusetts

EDUCATION: Harvard

PROFESSION: Merchant

AT YORK TOWN: September 30, 1777–
February 1, 1778
May 1778–June 28, 1778

Elbridge Gerry thoroughly understood and respected money. He knew how to earn it, he knew how to save it, and he knew how to spend it to make more money. Born the son and grandson of successful merchants, he never considered any career other than the family business—the exportation of dried codfish to Spain and Barbados.

By the time he was thirty-five, Gerry had amassed a tidy fortune in his own right. From 1774, when he worked with Samuel Adams and John Hancock on the Committee of Safety in charge of supplies, his knowledge of economics, his business know-how, and his natural shrewdness were valuable assets to the patriot cause.

On April 18, 1775, he had a narrow escape from the hangman. By hiding in a cornfield between Cambridge and Lexington, he eluded the British and, along with Adams and Hancock, shared the dubious distinction of being a man with "a price on his head." Elected to Congress in 1776, he signed the Declaration of Independence with a full knowledge of the risks involved. A serious little man, capable and self-confident, he had no time for frivolity and little appreciation for the bravado of his colleagues as expressed in the rash of jokes about being hanged. To him, it was no laughing matter, and he especially resented being twitted by the overweight Benjamin Harrison as to which of them would dangle longer from a British rope!

When he arrived at York Town, he was one of the fortunate five to secure lodgings at the comfortable home of General Daniel Roberdeau. He was also fortunate in being assigned to committees for which, by training and experience, he was well suited, especially the Committee of Commerce and the Treasury Board.

To understand the state of the revolutionary economy, it is useful to understand the meaning of the expression "not worth a Continental," which was the paper money printed by Congress without regard to the hard cash to back it. As an example of its utter worthlessness, it is recorded that a young delegate, while in Philadelphia, owed a bill of $21,373 for six months' lodging, plus $650 for the care of his horse. Small wonder that many delegates had to leave because they could not afford their positions! John Witherspoon was forced to take a leave of absence for that reason, Cornelius Harnett had spent more than a thousand dollars beyond his salary, and land-poor Francis Lightfoot Lee had to subsist mainly on pigeons purchased from local farmers while in York Town.

As measures of reform, Gerry recommended using every possible means for persuading the inhabitants of the various states to make loans for the support of the war. He also recommended more taxation and the printing of less paper currency. He was well aware of the revenue to be raised by the confiscation of Tory estates, but more strongly than he did with anything else, he implored Congress to exercise price controls across the nation. "It is evident," he wrote, "that trade will not regulate itself as to reduce the excessive prices of articles necessary to life . . . The partial attempt of a few states to restrain their inhabitants whilst those of the other states were permitted to make enormous fortunes must necessarily have produced the greatest uneasiness and created an opposition." Hence, in his opinion, the need for nationwide governmental regulation.

Elbridge Gerry has been accused by historians of frequent vacillation. This charge springs, in part, from his dealings with the military. Although a strong advocate of better pay and equipment, he wavered on the proposal for pensions. Opposed to a strong, standing army given the potential danger of a military take-over, he nonetheless advocated long-term enlistments.

His position on the Conway Cabal was just as ambivalent. A loyal champion of Washington, he befriended Conway at the same time. In answer to an inquiry from General Knox regarding intrigues against Washington, Gerry wrote, "I have not yet been able to make any discoveries that can justify a suspicion of a plan being formed to injure the reputation of, or remove from office, the Gentleman hinted at in your favor of January the 4th." And, as to the promotion of foreign officers over the heads of qualified Americans (an issue of great concern to the Commander-in-Chief), his expressed opinion was that the army was presently suffering from lack of experienced officers, and furthermore, he knew of "no promotions of any consequence that had not been made on the purest principles and full conviction of merit in the officer appointed."

Gerry continued to exercise the right to change his mind and party throughout his political career. As a member of the Constitutional Convention, he antagonized his fellows by "objecting to everything he did not propose." He refused to sign the Constitution and led the opposition to its ratification. Later, he changed his mind, supported it, and was elected to the First Congress. His haughty demeanor and quarrelsome nature cost him his popularity in Massachusetts, although he finally managed to serve two terms as Governor of the state. In 1787, he took his own advice and purchased a confiscated Tory property in Cambridge, where he lived the rest of his life. This house was later to become a landmark as the birthplace of the American poet and essayist James Russell Lowell.

The name of Elbridge Gerry will forever be associated with the term, GERRYMANDERING, meaning the redistricting of voting areas for political advantage. But the man himself deserves remembrance as a patriot to whom whatever, in his opinion, was in the best interest of his country was always first on his business agenda. It was while on his way to the Senate offices, as Vice President of the United States, that he suffered a fatal stroke. He is buried in the Congressional Cemetery in Washington, D.C.

The Paradoxical Patrioteer

JOHN HANCOCK

BIRTH: Quincy, Massachusetts
January 12, 1737

DEATH: Quincy, Massachusetts
October 8, 1793

COLONY: Massachusetts

EDUCATION: Boston Latin School, Harvard

OCCUPATION: Merchant

AT YORK TOWN: October 1, 1777–
October 29, 1777
June 19, 1778–
June 27, 1778

The life of John Hancock is a study in contradictions: A penniless orphan at seven, yet the wealthiest man in New England at twenty-seven; The son of a parson, but arrested as a smuggler; A loyal subject of the Crown, yet outlawed as a traitor; A lion of Boston's most elite Tory society, yet a boon companion of Samuel Adams and his radicals; Ridiculed by his enemies as a fop and a dandy, but cheered as a hero by the common people in their fight for freedom.

John Hancock was to follow this pattern of paradox all his life. Reared in the luxury of his uncle's Beacon Hill mansion and schooled as the heir to his mercantile empire, the young Hancock instinctively opposed Britain's oppressive tax measures that threatened the family business. The seizure of his sloop, *Liberty,* and his arrest for smuggling ashore its cargo of Madeira wine in 1768 unleashed such indignation, that almost overnight, he became a public figure. Defended by his boyhood friend John Adams, Hancock emerged from his lengthy and well-publicized trial as an idol of the populace and, thereafter, cast his lot with the patriots who welcomed his wealth and position as assets to their cause.

Elected Head of the Town Meeting, President of the Provincial Congress, and Chairman of the Committee of Safety, Hancock was a natural choice as delegate to the Second Continental Congress in 1775. His journey to Philadelphia—in the company of Sam and John Adams, Thomas Cushing, Robert Treat Paine, and the Connecticut delegation—amounted to a triumphal procession. Among the cheers of the crowds assembled along their route, the shouts for "KING HANCOCK" rang out louder than all the rest.

But the thirty-two-year-old patriot, was soon to have the chilling experience of "a hot friend cooling!" Although chosen to replace Peyton Randolph as President of Congress, the "Beau Brummel" of Boston found his popularity on the wane. His flamboyant dress, his princely bearing, his love of show and extravagant lifestyle, the very qualities that had endeared him to the public, were proving irksome to his fellow delegates. The first breach between Hancock and the Adamses occurred on June 4th, with the selection of a commander for the Continental Army. In a glowing speech deliberately calculated by John Adams to dupe the ambitious Hancock into believing that he was the candidate, Adams instead nominated George Washington. Describing the incident, Adams wrote:

I never marked a more sudden and sinking change of countenance. Mortification and resentment were expressed as forcibly as his face could exhibit them. Mr. Samuel Adams seconded the motion, and that did not soften the President's Phisiognomy at all.

In August of the same year, Hancock married the coquettish cousin of Abigail Adams, seventeen-year-old Dolly Quincy, whose presence enlivened the grueling months in Philadelphia and made their residence at Arch and Fourth Street a center of open-handed hospitality.

The vigorous boldness and confidence with which John Hancock signed the Declaration of Independence were inherent to his nature. Shortly, however, recurrent attacks of gout, fatigue, and grief at the loss of his baby daughter sapped his vitality in the days preceding the British occupation of Philadelphia. It was a bone-weary President who packed his wife off to Boston and fled with his Congress to York Town in September of 1777. On October 18th, he wrote to Dolly as follows:

I am now to inform you that I have come to a fixed determination to return to Boston for a short time and I have notified Congress in form of my intention.

Then came "the most unkindest cut of all." After his farewell speech of October 29th, in which he expressed his thanks for the "civility and politeness" he had received, his old comrade, Samuel

Adams, blocked the resolution "that the thanks of Congress be presented to John Hancock Esq. for the unremitted attention and impartiality he has manifested in discharge of the various duties of his office." In spite of opposition from New Hampshire, Massachusetts, Rhode Island, and Pennsylvania, the resolution was finally passed, but John Hancock neither forgave nor forgot.

Delaying his departure from Dolly until after the birth of their son, Hancock did not return to York Town until the week before Congress adjourned to Philadelphia in June. But in the interim, he had spent $25,000 for the printing and distribution of 400,000 pamphlets entitled *Your Articles of Confederation,* urging their early ratification.

Contrary to the mixed feelings he aroused in Congress, from which he took his final leave in 1780, Hancock's popularity in his home state never diminished. Nine times he was elected Governor, and in 1778, he presided over the convention for the adoption of the Federal Constitution. In American history, John Hancock's signature eclipses the man himself, his image obscured by conflicting elements.

Among his other paradoxes, he was a prominent businessman, yet his accounts as treasurer of Harvard College were so mishandled that they were not completely settled until after his death. He was a dedicated leader of his state but known to avoid unpopular decisions by "convenient attacks of gout." He was envious and resentful of the first President, yet he named his only son *John George Washington Hancock.* He was generous in his financial support of the Revolution, but he billed Congress for such trifling items as "Cash paid for paper, ink, wax, and tape."

Broken in health and shattered by the tragic death of his nine-year-old son, John Hancock died at the beginning of his ninth term as Governor. Twenty thousand people marched in his funeral procession, the grandest ever seen in Boston. Representatives from every branch of local, state, and national government; envoys from foreign countries; the Boston clergy; officers of the militia; professors of Harvard College; as well as throngs of his fellow citizens joined in the final tribute. Among the mourners were John Adams, who had defeated him for the Vice Presidency, and Samuel Adams, who would succeed him as Governor. At the gravesite in the Old Granary Burying Ground, the traditional funeral dirges gave way to the lively strains of "Yankee Doodle." It was to this stirring and highly appropriate air that the body of John Hancock became forever a part of New England's unyielding soil.

A Yankee Diarist

SAMUEL HOLTEN

BIRTH: Salem Village (Danvers),
　　　　Massachusetts
　　　　January 9, 1738

DEATH: Danvers, Massachusetts
　　　　January 2, 1816

COLONY: Massachusetts

EDUCATION: Medicine

PROFESSION: Physician

AT YORK TOWN: June 22, 1778–
　　　　　　　　June 27, 1778

When Samuel Holten presented his credentials and took his seat in Congress on Monday, June 22, 1778, he found that body in a jovial mood. The long-awaited day of returning to Philadelphia was at last in sight. On Saturday, June 27th, it was moved to adjourn until the following Thursday, July 2nd, when they would reassemble in Philadelphia.

Samuel Holten's parents, Samuel and Hannah Gardner Holten, had hoped to give their son a college education, but the strain of preparation was deemed too much for the boy's ill health. Instead, he studied with Dr. Jonathan Price and became a doctor, starting a practice in Gloucester in 1756, where he met and married Mary Warner. The couple then returned to Danvers, where his practice of medicine and his friendly nature won him a wide circle of friends in the community. This resulted in his being sent to the General Court in 1768 and serving in one public office after the other until the year before his death. As his interest in public affairs—most especially in the Revolutionary cause—increased, his interest in medicine diminished, and he became a popular politician.

His service in Congress, which began at York Town, continued throughout most of the years between the Articles of Confederation and the formation of the government under the new Constitution.

During his first year in Congress, Holten kept a diary from which he deliberately omitted any and all reference to public affairs. Nonetheless, the entries do provide a picture of his life and times. They are extremely brief and to the point. The first one from York Town, dated June 22nd, reads as follows: "I took my seat in Congress, and it is a very August Assembly." That of the following day was a bit more informative: "Attended in Congress and the chief of the day was taken up in Disputing on the Articles of Confederation." The "disputing" he refers to concerned the debate and ultimate rejection of amendments suggested by the Maryland, Massachusetts, Rhode Island, and Connecticut delegations.

The last notations written in York Town were on June 24th, when he "Attended in Congress, dined with the President, and Congress did not sit in the afternoon," and on June 25th, when he:

> Attended in Congress. Towards night, I walked out with a number of Gentlemen from Congress about a mile, to farm house. The people was kind, we eat Charies [cherries] and Drank whiskey.

That he was unaccustomed to Pennsylvania's summer weather is apparent in his entry of June 26th. "Attended in Congress and it is the hottest day I ever knew. Went and drank tea with the President & drank tea with the Secretary." From June 27th to July 1st, the diary covers the journey from York Town to Philadelphia. It can be noted that whatever instruction he may have received in medicine, spelling instruction had been woefully neglected.

> June 27, 1778: "Attended in Congress in the forenoon and they adjourned to the city of Philada. to meet on Thursday next 10 o'clock."
> June 28, 1788: "Sabbath Day. Travd. from York Town. Crossed the Susquehanna 20 miles lower than where I did before. Dined at a good inn but have a small room to lodge in this night. N.B. and the bugs drove us out."

> June 29, 1778: "Travd. 12 miles before brakfast, brakfasted on whartlebary—still outdoors, then travd 7 miles, dined at good inn, then travd 15 miles to Newart in one of the lower counties in Delaware State."
> June 30, 1778: "Travd. from Newart to Wilmanton 11 miles, had brakfast and dined; we passed thro' part of the State of Maryland, & Wilmanton is a principal town in the State of Delaware. The building are chiefly Bricke and very commodious. We then travd. to Chester where we are likely to be well accomodated."
> July 1, 1778: "Travd. to the city of Philadelhia 15 miles before brakfast. Dined at a public house. Then took lodgings at the wido Robinson's in Chestnut Street."

Congress was unable to summon a quorum until July 7th, but in an informal session, a decision was reached pertaining to the July 4th celebration of Independence, which was published in the July 3rd edition of Dunlap's *Pennsylvania Packet.* Citizens were advised against illuminating their homes on that occasion because of the scarcity of candles, a measure that did not diminish Samuel Holten's pleasure in the event:

> The Congress dined together at the City Tavern & a number of the Council of this State, several Genl. Officers and other Gentn of Distinction, & while we were dining there was an agreeable Band of Musick, and we had a very elegant dinner.

Holten's medical knowledge was put to good use in Congress, where he served on committees involving medical and surgical supplies for the army. Although he did not resume practice after his return to Danvers, he was influential in the founding of the Massachusetts Medical Society in 1781. He must have outgrown the ill health that plagued him as a youth, because he lived to the age of seventy-eight as a respected and well-loved patriarch of his native state.

JAMES LOVELL

BIRTH: Boston, Massachusetts
October 31, 1737

DEATH: Windham, Maine
July 14, 1814

COLONY: Massachusetts

EDUCATION: Harvard

OCCUPATION: Schoolmaster

AT YORK TOWN: October 1, 1777–
June 27, 1778

James Lovell came honestly by his talent for criticism. With eighteen years of experience as an usher in Boston's famous South Grammar School, where his father, John Lovell, was Head Master, he was accustomed to making authoritative judgments about the young Bostonians under his tutelage. Furthermore, his excellent command of English and his fluency in French and Latin enabled him to express his opinions in three languages.

Aside from continuing in the teaching profession, James did not follow in his father's footsteps. John Lovell was a STAUNCH Loyalist, but his son an ardent patriot. In April of 1775, the Grammar School was closed by British authority. "War's come—school's done," announced Master Lovell, who shortly afterward took refuge in Halifax, Nova Scotia.

In February of 1777, when Lovell first took his seat, Congress had evacuated Philadelphia and was meeting in a rented house in Baltimore. A single room was large enough to accommodate a sadly depleted membership. A slim Congress made a heavy workload, however, and James Lovell soon earned a reputation for unflagging energy. Describing a similar situation during the winter of 1778, when Congress was again working at half-strength, Elbridge Gerry observed:

> Few can stand it as well as our friend Mr. Lovell;
> he writes Morning, Noon and Night; sickens once

a fortnight, and devotes a day to sleep, after which, like the Sun from behind a cloud, he makes his appearance with his usual splendor.

Except for such brief bouts with illness, which while in York Town he ascribed to the "lime water," claiming it had torn many of his countrymen's bowels out, Lovell was seldom absent. During the entire five years of his service, he never once visited his family and was openly scornful of those who timed their attendance to suit their personal comfort and convenience. Like Thomas Paine, he had little use for the "Sunshine Patriot." After a "sad winter's campaign in York Town," he wrote to Samuel Adams in April of 1778, "we are now come to the season when certain birds of passage return who seldom appear in our flock during the winter."

A self-styled "quill driver," Lovell's correspondence was both lively and voluminous. His personal letters are highly seasoned with pithy observations and often so sprinkled with abbreviations and nicknames as to require as glossary. A cryptic communiqué to Arthur Lee in 1779 serves as an example:

> W.H.D. is off the Stage . . . Jimmy D. and Gov. M. are behind the scenes; Judge F-l and Woody L-don are on their pillows. But the main Chair is full. The Farmer the Fidler and the Boatswain are active.

Thus was Lee informed that William Henry Drayton had died, James Duane and Gouverneur Morris were absent; John Fell and Woodbury Langdon were ill, and President John Jay was presiding over a meeting where John Dickinson, Meriwether Lewis, and William Carmichael were up to some skullduggery.

Nevertheless, there was nothing cryptic about Lovell's relentless criticism of Silas Deane, whose indiscriminate recruitment of volunteers with irresponsible promises of high rank frequently placed Congress in the embarrassing position of elevating foreigners above experienced American officers. Infuriated by this continued "slight" to his countrymen, Lovell worked incessantly to have the "weak or roguish man" recalled from his French post.

Meanwhile, his assignment as interpreter to the non–English-speaking volunteers became more and more irksome. "These Frenchmen," he wrote to Joseph Trumbull in June of 1777, "have used me quite up!" And again, "These contending, endless talkers and writers have entirely destroyed me!"

An officer of Lafayette's party, arriving in Philadelphia on July 27th, recorded an account of the cool reception:

> M [Mr. Lovell] talked with us in the street where he left us, having treated us, in excellent French, like a set of adventurers. He ended his speech by saying . . . 'It seems the French officers have a great fancy to enter our service without being invited.'

Fortunately for the course of American history, Lafayette ignored the rebuff and presented his case directly to the President of Congress, with the result that four days later, he was commissioned as a Major General in the American Army.

But Lovell's caustic barbs were soon to find another target. His extravagant admiration for General Gates, especially after the victory at Saratoga, inspired his most scathing comments on Washington's "consummate and repeated blundering." Writing from York Town in an atmosphere charged with mistrust and discouragement, he freely vented his hostility toward the Commander-in-Chief. "A Demi-God," he called him. "One great Man whom no citizen shall dare to even talk about!" Ridiculing his reluctance to attack Howe, he accused Washington of "marching his army up and down with no other purpose than to wear out their clothing, shoes, and stockings!" He firmly believed, as he wrote to Gates, "This army will be totally lost unless you come down and collect the virtuous band who wish to fight under your banner, and with their aid save the Southern hemisphere."

Still, despite his causticity, this salty New Englander was as devoted as any man of his time to the American cause. His reaction to the British Commissioners' peace proposals of 1778 was brief and blunt: "They do not allow Independence; therefore they might have tarried at home!"

Whatever ambitions James Lovell may have had for a career in foreign affairs were doomed by his personal lack of diplomacy, but his criticisms, however harsh, were born of honest convictions. His integrity was never questioned. The key to his character may be found in the concluding paragraph of one of his many diatribes against the unfortunate Deane:

> In short I write because I had determined it to be my Duty so to write. That Path once determined, I never ask myself whether there may not be a Lion in the way!

NEW HAMPSHIRE

Bartlett, Josiah
Folsom, Nathaniel
Frost, George
Wentworth, John

Proclamation Line of 1763

MA

NY MA

PA RI

CT

NJ

MD DE

VA

NC

SC

GA

The Double-Duty Delegate

JOSIAH BARTLETT

BIRTH: Amesbury, Massachusetts
November 21, 1729

DEATH: Kingston, New Hampshire
May 19, 1795

COLONY: New Hampshire

EDUCATION: Tutors

PROFESSION: Physician

AT YORK TOWN: May 21, 1778–
July 2, 1778

Josiah Bartlett left New Hampshire for York Town May 5, 1778 and arrived on the morning of May 21st. This was not his first journey to Pennsylvania. He was a member of both the first and second Continental Congress and was the first delegate to cast his vote for independence . . . second only to John Hancock to affix his signature to the Declaration of Independence.

History portrays Bartlett as a loyal patriot, an able politician, a distinguished judge, and a successful physician. But his letters to his wife reveal him as a devoted husband, loving father, and a warm, caring individual. These same letters provide close-ups, homely bits, and pieces of the revolutionary scene not to be found in official records.

Bartlett wrote to his family about anything and everything of possible interest to them and of personal importance to him. As a father and a physician, his main concern was their health and well-being. The condition of his ailing daughter, Rhoda, was always uppermost in his mind. One of his letters throws some light on his medical theories and practices:

> My opinion is that proper exercise, air and diet, and to keep the mind as easy and contented as possible in such disorders, is of more service than a multiplicity of medicines. Tho, no doubt, some would be useful.

Naturally, his own comforts and discomforts would have been of interest to the folks at home:

Have found lodging at a German House about a quarter of a mile from the Court House where the Congress sets. His name is Andrus Hoffman. Their manner of cooking their victuals is very different from the English Manner, tho they do what they can to accommodate us. They understand but little English, just enough to be understood.

And, of course, there was always the weather report:

The weather here is very seasonable—not over hot and rather wet than dry.

But, by far, the most sensational report is dated June 28th:

We happened to have sight of the Eclipse of the Sun last Wednesday; it was so cloudy all Monday and Tuesday and Wednesday till about 8 o'clock in the morning that the Sun did not once appear. Afterwards, the clouds broke so that we had a pretty good sight of it. It was much the largest Eclipse I ever saw. It was all covered except a very small rim at the Northwest, smaller than the bright part of the Moon when she first appears after the change. The weather here now is very hot and has been so for three days past.

In spite of the pressure of state business, he was always interested in conditions at home, especially that of the crops:

I want to know how hay is likely to be with us; how the English corn is like to be, whether the worms destroy the Indian corn, how the flax is like to turn out, etc., etc., etc.

And again:

I am sorry to hear there is likely to be a scarcity of Cider, as I sensibly feel the want of it here, where there is always a Scarcity or rather where they never use much of it, and what is made, is very inferior to the New England Cider; If I am not likely to make any, I hope you will purchase a few barrels, as I should be glad of a little after so long fasting from it.

There was nothing too trivial to claim his attention—Sally's cold, Levi's studies, a promise to Peter ("If he behaves himself, I will remember my promise."), and even the outcome of the lottery:

I can now inform you and my children that there will be no difficulty in dividing our Prize money from the Lottery as every one of the tickets in our family are BLANKS!

He also kept his family abreast of the news—the rejection of Lord North's peace proposals, the arrival of the French treaties, and the long-awaited removal to Philadelphia. But York Town must, indeed, have been a paradise when compared with the devastated Philadelphia as described by Bartlett:

In addition to 'a plague of flies', the State House was left by the enemy in a most filthy and sordid condition, as were many of the public and private buildings in the city. Some of the genteel houses were used as stables and holes cut in the parlor floors and their dung shoveled into the cellars. The country Northward of the City for several miles is one common waste, the houses burnt, the fruit trees and others cut down and carried off, fences carried away, gardens and orchards destroyed—Mr. Dickenson's and Mr. Morris' fine seats all demolished.

Nevertheless, the irrepressible Bartlett found lighter subjects with which to regale the female members of his household—namely, the fashions:

When the Congress first moved into the City, they found the Tory Ladies who lingered with the regulars, wearing the most enormous high Head-dresses, after the manner of the Mistresses and Wh--es of the British Officers. The Head-dresses are now shortening, and the little bobbed hats for the men are growing fast out of fashion. The mode now is large, round, brims, and cocked nearly three-square, no hats are made in any other mode here. So much for fashions, for the satisfaction of my children.

To add to his discomfort and general misery, Charles Chase, his faithful manservant, was taken very ill and had to be visited twice a day. This illness, plus the indisposition of his colleague, John Wentworth, left him completely without help. He was doing a double job as doctor and nurse and performing double duty as a delegate.

Josiah Bartlett was an American patriot of many responsibilities and the fortitude to bear them all with good grace—husband and father, doctor and nurse, farmer and statesman, Signer of the Declaration of Independence and Articles of Confederation, and first governor of New Hampshire under the new constitution. Few men have crowded more and varied services into sixty-five years of living as did Josiah Bartlett.

Man of Granite

NATHANIEL FOLSOM

BIRTH: Exeter, New Hampshire
September 18, 1726

DEATH: Exeter, New Hampshire
May 26, 1790

COLONY: New Hampshire

EDUCATION: Public schools

PROFESSION: Military, Major General,
Chief Justice

AT YORK TOWN: September 30, 1777–
January 1778

Nathaniel Folsom was among those who fled the British advance on Philadelphia in 1777. The question of adjournment had been discussed in Congress almost daily throughout the month of September but was always over-ruled. However, during the night of September 18, a warning from Colonel Alexander Hamilton that the British were about to cross the Schuylkill River precipitated their flight. The Loyalist Press made much of the hastiness of their departure. A Tory teenager, Robert Morton, noted in his diary that Hamilton's warning had:

> so much alarmed the Gentlemen of the Congress, the military officers and other friends, the general cause of American freedom and independence that decamped with the utmost precipitation, and in the greatest confusion, inasmuch that one of the delegates, by name of Nathaniel Fulsom of New Hampshire was obliged in a very fulsome manner to ride off without a saddle.

Whether the lack of saddle was because of haste or because, as a New England farm boy, he was accustomed to riding bareback, only Folsom could answer.

Folsom had neither the education nor the inclination to become a statesman, but his character was as firm and unyielding as the rock for which his state is named. A man of granite he proved to be in his opposition to the manner of computing taxation as set forth in the Articles of Confederation. He vigorously argued against using land value as the basis of taxation, claiming, as did all the New England delegates, that the omission of slaves in assessing the wealth of the Southern states was grossly unfair. Even after the Articles were completed, printed, and sent out for ratification, he persisted in his efforts for change.

Folsom's letters make interesting reading, not only for their content but also for their unusual and highly creative spelling. His outrage over the perfidy of the Reverend Duche, who had prayed so eloquently for the Cause in 1774 only to betray it in 1777, caused him to express indignation to his friend, Josiah Bartlett:

> I inclose you a Coppey of a letter from the Revt. Mr. Ducha to General Washington that you may see what a Judas wase a Chaplin of Congress. Wood not have you make it Publick unless it be by advice of Councile. Congress have not seen fir th Publish it here, tho it is Publick anough in everybodey's mouth i the Streets.

But even men of granite have their periods of frustration and fatigue. In October, Folsom was beginning to feel the pressure. "My Duty is Very hard," he wrote Bartlett, "and if you have any Compashion left for me, I hope you will Joyne Congress soone, as this business is too much for me to live (with)."

As fall faded into winter, the pressure mounted. Folsom realized that the actions of Congress were not always inspired by the best of motives. In response to Bartlett's criticism of the promotion of Colonel James Wilkinson to the rank of Brigadier General, he voiced his disillusionment and disgust (as to this promotion):

> Which you say has given you pain I most Sincerely Sympothise with you, and can say it has given men Sebceble Pain every since it was Done. I was glad he asked no more at that time, for assured I am that if he had, it would have been granted.

And, as his letter continued, he further charged Congress with favoritism, which was rapidly undermining both the army and its commander. Officers were being appointed, as it seemed to him:

> more upon the Principle of Interest and Friendship than Justice and Equitey. Grate uneasiness in the Army has been the Sure and sertaine Consequence of the appointment of every general Officer Since I have been here.

There was also a strong suggestion of injured feelings over Bartlett's criticism:

> If you mean me Personally Considerd, and think you could do better, hope you will, in twenty four hours after recieving this, mount your horse and Come and Reliev me. And if you think you cant Do so well, would not have that Stop you as I have wrone allmost all the flesh off my Bones being Exercised in my Mind night and day and no time to Relax.

His fear of being left alone at York Town over the winter was never realized. In late January, he was assigned to the Committee on Army Reorganization at Camp (Valley Forge) to assess the exact state and condition of the Army and the feasibility of a surprise attack on Philadelphia. Because this was a plan initiated by Congress, they were greatly disappointed by the report, signed by Francis Dana, John Reed, John Harvie, Gouverneur Morris, and Nathaniel Folsom. The committee ruled the venture both impractical and dangerous because of the inadequacy in numbers and poor physical condition of the troops, insufficient supplies, uncertainty of the weather and treacherous state of the Schuylkill (which Congress expected the army to cross by way of the ice), and the likelihood of a disastrous failure.

Nathaniel Folsom retired from Congress permanently in 1782, but served as the President of New Hampshire's Constitutional Convention the following year. For his personal sacrifices and dedication, this hard-working, strong-minded man deserves the acclaim of his fellow countrymen.

An Old Salt

GEORGE FROST

BIRTH: New Castle, New Hampshire
April 26, 1720

DEATH: Durham, New Hampshire
June 21, 1796

COLONY: New Hampshire

EDUCATION: Common School

PROFESSION: Seaman, Jurist

AT YORK TOWN: December 8, 1777–
April 1, 1778

It is highly probable that George Frost inherited his love for the sea from his father, John Frost, who was a commander in the British navy. John Frost died when George was only twelve years old, leaving him to be reared by his uncle, Sir William Pepperell of Kittery Point, New Hampshire. Having already obtained a common-school education, George was trained in his uncle's counting house, where he showed early promise of a mercantile career. When he was twenty, George put to sea in one of Pepperell's ships, of which he later became captain. At some point he decided to put his nautical and mercantile skills together in a different manner, one that was known to be both lucrative and dangerous. He became a privateer. His action, in an incipient manner, may have helped to steer the ship of his career toward both politics and serving one's country, for in 1760, while master of the ship aptly named *Enterprise,* George Frost was awarded the King's Commission to go hunt and capture French shipping as an extended part of the war we refer to as the French and Indian War.

Frost, by that time only a middle-aged "salt," must also have had an adventurous streak, for, after all, privateering was merely a legalized form of piracy! Frost followed his sea-faring career for twenty years, during which time he formed a partnership with George Richards of London, England.

When George bade farewell to the sea, he returned to his old home in New Castle. He lived there until his marriage in 1764 and subsequently moved to Durham. There, he discovered as many, if not more, opportunities awaiting him on land as at sea. Some of his pursuits were far more grounded in prosperity than during his seafaring days. He first served his community as Justice of the Peace in 1773, the same year he became Judge of Common Pleas for Stafford County, serving from 1773 to 1791, and several of those years in the capacity of Chief Justice. It was during this period that he was elected to the Continental Congress. Frost also became a member of his state's Governor's Council, where he served from 1781 until 1784.

At York Town, he brought his personal experience and knowledge into play by serving on the Maritime Committee, which could not boast any other ex–sea captains among its members. Hard work and dedication not only helped George Frost pilot his own ship of life to a safe harbor, it also helped him to guide the Ship of State through the storm-tossed seas of the American Revolution.

JOHN WENTWORTH

BIRTH: Somersworth, New Hampshire
July 17, 1745

DEATH: Dover, New Hampshire
January 10, 1787

COLONY: New Hampshire

EDUCATION: Harvard

PROFESSION: Lawyer

AT YORK TOWN: May 21, 1778–
July 1778

When John Wentworth left New Hampshire with his colleague, Josiah Bartlett, May 5, 1778, he had the potential of serving his state as an articulate, conscientious delegate. As a lawyer with experience in the Legislature, he was well qualified for the role. But he was not prepared for contracting smallpox. While still in New York, he and his aide began to show symptoms of the dreaded disease. In his capacity of physician, Bartlett promptly inoculated both men, but it was too late. They were able to continue their journey to York Town only as far as Reading, Pennsylvania. Declaring him unfit for travel, Dr. Bartlett left him there in the care of his servant.

Congress accepted the credentials of both New Hampshire delegates on May 21, 1778, but only Bartlett took his seat. It was not until May 30, 1778, that Wentworth was able to share the table with his fellow delegate from the Granite State. He secured lodgings with Bartlett and was able to attend Congress for most of the month. However, he fell ill again and was in such a poor state of health by the time Congress was ready to adjourn to Philadelphia that he was unable to accompany them. Dr. Bartlett also remained in York Town to care for his friend until it was finally safe for him to be left alone. Bartlett then heard nothing more of his patient until July 20th, when a report from Hannah Thomson, wife of Secretary Thomson, stated that Wentworth had had a serious relapse. In early August, Wentworth finally arrived in Philadelphia, but was still too sick to attend Congress. "If he does not get well soon," wrote Bartlett, "I suppose he will set out for home," and he was right. The unfortunate Wentworth left Philadelphia on August 21st and arrived home safely on September 11th. The bill he submitted to the New Hampshire government covered 132 days at 30 shillings per day.

John Wentworth regained his health in New Hampshire, where, surprisingly enough, he was able to serve as Register of Probate until his death nine years later. That he was Delegate to Congress "in name only" is attested to by a letter from Josiah Bartlett to Governor Meshech Weare:

[I] must beg leave to inform you that I can by no means attend Congress after the last of October next. By reason of Mr. Wentworth's sickness, I have not received the least assistance from him, and am obliged to attend so closely to public business, without any interval of relaxation, that it will be necessary for my constitution of body and mind to be relieved then, if I am able to hold out till that time.

I hope, Sir, that you will give Mr. Whipple & Frost notice, and that they will be here seasonable, as the State will not be represented.

NEW JERSEY

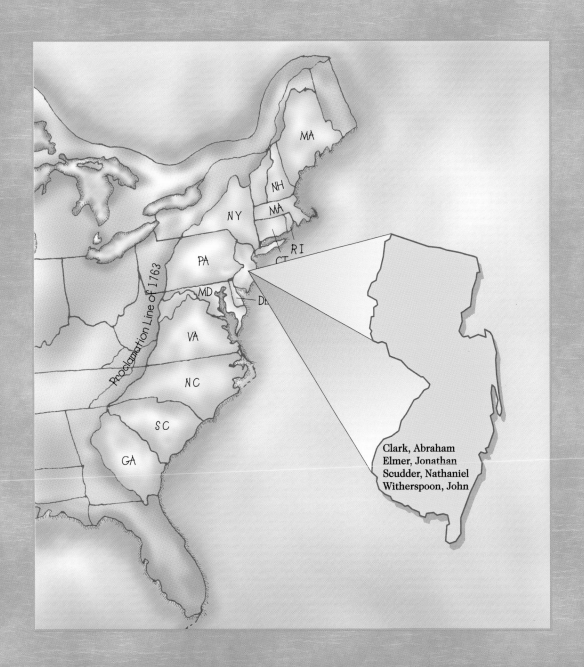

MA

NH

NY
MA

PA
RI
CT

MD
DE

VA

Proclamation Line of 1763

NC

SC

GA

Clark, Abraham
Elmer, Jonathan
Scudder, Nathaniel
Witherspoon, John

The Poor Man's Counselor

ABRAHAM CLARK

BIRTH: Elizabethtown, New Jersey
February 15, 1726

DEATH: Rahway, New Jersey
September 15, 1794

COLONY: New Jersey

EDUCATION: Self-taught

PROFESSION: Farmer, Surveyor, Lawyer

AT YORK TOWN: December 11, 1777–
March 7, 1778

When Abraham Clark signed the Declaration of Independence, he did so not merely because of his instructions from New Jersey but largely because of a deep personal faith in one of the document's basic truths—that all men are created equal. They are, therefore, afforded equal access and protection of the law, not limited by costly legal fees. He, himself, was a product of this philosophy.

Born the only child of a farming family, but too frail to do much heavy work, his educational opportunities were mostly of his own making. He had a natural curiosity about numbers and how they worked, so he explored the field of mathematics and gained sufficient mastery of the subject to become a surveyor. Later, he began the study of civil law to handle land agreements and general business transactions. As his knowledge increased, he shared it with his neighbors, offering them the benefit of counsel without charge or for the exchange of produce and other commodities—thus, his honorary title of COUNSELOR TO THE POOR. Although never formally admitted to the Bar, he practiced law in New Jersey and, despite an abundance of pro bono work, was able to make a living for himself, his wife, and his ten children.

Like his father, he was never too busy to take part in civic affairs. He represented the Crown in several public offices, but by 1774, he was active on the Committee of Public Safety and a member of the Provincial Assembly. In June of 1776, he was sent to Continental Congress, committed to independence.

Abraham Clark presented his credentials to the Congress of York Town on December 11, 1777, at a time crucial both to his state and to Congress as a whole. New Jersey had been without representation since the departure of Jonathan Elmer on November 20th. President Laurens had been instructed to write to Governor Livingston, asking him to remedy this situation, but he refrained from doing so because of Clark's welcome arrival and the promise of John Witherspoon's attendance.

Clark found Congress besieged by several weighty problems, and he became personally concerned over the inefficiency of the Commissary Department, the suffering of the troops at Valley Forge, and the antagonism of the Board of War against Washington. This last issue threatened to split Congress into two camps.

A letter to General William Alexander, dated January 15, 1777, clearly outlines the circumstances that history later refers to as the Conway Cabal, naming General Gates and James Wilkinson among those involved. This same letter also gives a comprehensive survey of the State of the Union, the uncertainty of the final settlement of the Saratoga Convention, the possibility of war between France and Britain, and "the indolence, ignorance, disaffection or avarice of the Commissaries."

Fortunately for Clark's peace of mind, he was appointed, together with Elbridge Gerry and Jonathan Bayard Smith, to investigate the commissariat system and "to report such alterations therein as they shall deem best calculated to answer the end of the institution."

Clark continued to serve in Congress and his state legislature until the end of the war. His concerns for his country were equaled—and even surpassed—by his anxieties for home and family, which were in constant danger from the enemy. In fact, two of his sons were captured by the English and held captive on the British prison ship *Jersey*.

Clark's productive and useful life was cut short on a hot September day in 1794. He suffered severe sunstroke which proved to be fatal two hours later. Although the name Abraham Clark has never been listed among our national heroes, he deserves to be honored as one who spent his life in the service of his fellow man and his country.

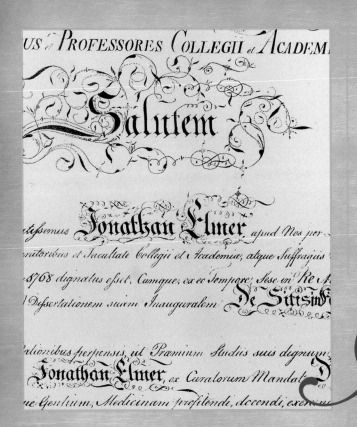

The Little Doctor

JONATHAN ELMER

BIRTH: Cumberland County, New Jersey
November 29, 1745

DEATH: Bridgeton, New Jersey
September 3, 1817

COLONY: New Jersey

EDUCATION: Medical School, University
of Pennsylvania

PROFESSION: Physician

AT YORK TOWN: October 14, 1777–
November 21, 1777
May 26, 1778–
May 31, 1778

The Elmer brothers, Jonathan and Ebeneezer, were not twins, but their careers bore a remarkable resemblance to each other. Both were doctors, and they shared an office in which they published their joint newspaper, *The Plain Dealer*. Both were also members of Congress. Jonathan was seven years older than his brother, and in 1765, he was a member of the first medical class ever to be graduated from the University of Pennsylvania. He set up a practice in Bridgeton (or Bridge Town, as it was called at that time), New Jersey. There, he married Mary Seeley, and the couple later built a large frame house that doubled as a home and an office.

In 1775, the two brothers formed an association for the publication of New Jersey's first newspaper. The following year, each saw service in the Continental army. Although Jonathan's main interest was medicine, he held several public offices, and his sentiments for the revolutionary cause were sufficiently known for him to be elected to the Continental Congress in 1776. His final act before leaving for that post was to read the Declaration of Independence to his fellow townsmen, after which they burned the King's Coat of Arms as a gesture of defiance.

Probably the best summary of Jonathan Elmer's congressional credo is to be found in a letter that he wrote the day before he left York Town:

I have made it my business ever since I have had the honour of a seat in Congress, to attend as constantly as possible. Whether I have discharged the important trust reposed in me by my constituents to their satisfaction or not, I leave them to judge. I can now, ever with truth, declare that I have at all times exerted myself to the utmost of my slender abilities for the good of my country and in particular, of the state which I have had the honour of representing.

With the conclusion of his congressional duties, he returned to the practice of medicine and was elected President of the Medical Society of New Jersey, but his political career was not over. He was elected to the U.S. Senate under the new Constitution as a Federalist in 1789 and served through 1791. In an article by Bill Chestnut, appearing in *South Jersey Magazine,* one of his fellow senators is quoted as saying, "I know not in the Senate a man, if I were to choose a friend on whom I would cast the eye of confidence as soon as on this little Doctor."

During the last twenty-five years of his life, Elmer devoted himself to his medical practice and to the Presbyterian Church, where he served as an Elder and a Delegate to the Presbytery and General Assembly. He lived to see his younger brother, Ebeneezer, become a member of the 7th, 8th, and 9th Congress of the United States. He also would have been proud to know that his nephew, Lucius Quintus Cincinnatus Elmer, served in the 28th Congress of the United States.

Jonathan Elmer, considered one of the most distinguished patriots of New Jersey, is buried outside the historic Old Broad Street Church of Bridge Town, where his tomb bears an epitaph reflecting the love and admiration of his fellow citizens:

HERE LIES
IN HOPE OF
A GLORIOUS RESURRECTION
THE BODY OF
JONATHAN ELMER, M.D.
AND FELLOW OF THE
AMERICAN PHILOSOPHICAL AND CIVILIAN
A DISTINGUISHED CITIZEN AND
AN EXEMPLARY CHRISTIAN
WHO DEPARTED THIS LIFE SEPTEMBER 3, 1817
IN THE 72 YEAR OF HIS AGE.
ATTEMPT NOT ON MARBLE TO PORTRAY
A LIFE WELL SPENT IS MAN'S BEST EPITAPH
THAT LIFE'S WELL SPENT
WHICH ANSWERS LIFE'S GREAT END.

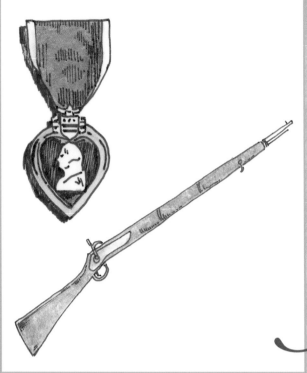

NATHANIEL SCUDDER

BIRTH: Long Island, New York
      May 10, 1733

DEATH: New Jersey
      October 17, 1781

COLONY: New Jersey

EDUCATION: College of New Jersey
      (Princeton University)

PROFESSION: Physician

AT YORK TOWN: February 9, 1778–
      May 23, 1778
      June 19, 1778–
      June 27, 1778

On February 2, 1778, John Witherspoon wrote to his friend, Dr. Benjamin Rush, that he would soon see him at Princeton. He was planning to go home as soon as Dr. Nathaniel Scudder arrived to take his place. Dr. Scudder did arrive, a week later, taking his seat in Congress on February 9th. A physician with a large practice in the area of Monmouth County, Scudder was a welcome addition to the Congress of 1778. He was not only a well-educated man but also an ardent and active patriot since the very beginning of the Revolution. He had served as Lieutenant Colonel of the First Regiment of the Monmouth New Jersey Militia and, in 1777, had been promoted to full Colonel of that regiment. At the same time, he was an active member of the Council of Safety. On November 30th, he was elected as a delegate to Congress.

While in Congress, Scudder worked long and hard to persuade his state to ratify the Articles of Confederation. He pointed out to the General Assembly of New Jersey that, without ratification by all thirteen colonies, we would remain "an unconfederated people, unable to treat with foreign powers on an equal national footing." He also emphasized the potential dangers from Great Britain, which would likely take advantage of such disunion. "For my own part," he wrote, "I am of opinion she will never desist from her nefarious designs, nor ever consider her attempts upon our liberties fruitless and vain, until she knows the Golden Knot is actually tied."

However, it was not until March 1, 1780, that a ratification celebration was held for the much disputed Articles as completed by the Congress in York Town on November 15, 1777.

In the fall of 1781, Dr. Scudder was again in the service of the Monmouth New Jersey Militia. In an engagement with British troops and Tories at Black's Point, Nathaniel Scudder was killed while leading a battalion of his regiment. He had the distinction of being the only member of Congress to lose his life in battle during the Revolutionary War.

In an affectionate letter to his son, Joseph, written at York Town on May 1, 1778, Nathaniel Scudder revealed his hopes and dreams of the future, "a future of new promise, opportunity and challenge of the brave New World" that his generation of courageous patriots had helped to create:

A scene is opening, my dear Child, in this Country for the greatest imaginable display of Talents and Education, and a young man with your capacity, abilities and learning, can't fail, under God, if he sets out right, of making a figure in Public Life on the great Stage of this New World. Indeed, I cannot help contemplating my sons as shining in future in some of the most splendid Departments of this mighty, rising American Empire, the Glory of the Western World.

A Persuasive Presbyterian

JOHN WITHERSPOON

BIRTH: Gifford, Haddingtonshire, Scotland
February 5, 1732

DEATH: Princeton, NJ
November 15, 1794

COLONY: New Jersey

EDUCATION: University of Edinburgh

PROFESSION: Clergyman

AT YORK TOWN: September 1777–
October 1777
December 17, 1777–
January 31, 1778
May 16, 1778–
June 28, 1778

As a minister, John Witherspoon was a master of the art of persuasion, but when he was invited to accept the presidency of the College of New Jersey, which later became Princeton, it took him two years to persuade his wife to leave their home in Scotland. She was terrified of crossing the ocean, and to her, America was an uncharted wilderness. However, they eventually set sail with their five children and three hundred donated books that he had persuaded his congregation to contribute.

When Witherspoon arrived at Princeton, he found the college in such bad financial shape that he toured New England and other nearby colonies persuading fellow Presbyterians to make financial contributions to the college. Under his administration, the school expanded, and the curriculum was greatly enriched.

With a Scotsman's innate distrust of the English, Witherspoon's voice was soon raised in strong support of resistance to the Crown and was responsible for persuading most of the Scotch-Irish population to join the American cause. His spirit of Independence was reflected in the student body, and by 1774, the campus became a hotbed of rebellion. Not only did the students burn the winter's supply of tea, but the commencement address of that year was a fervent plea for action.

By 1776, John Witherspoon was New Jersey's natural choice for representative in Congress. He took his seat there on July 2nd in time to make an impassioned speech, declaring that the colonies were "not only ripe for independence, they were in danger of rotting for want of it." New Jersey's position was assured.

During his stint at York Town, Witherspoon's powers of persuasion were put to good use. He proved to be a shrewd debator on details of the Articles of Confederation and a canny diplomat when Burgoyne's surrender to Gates at Saratoga threatened to turn from a "glorious" to a "Pyrrhic victory." Flushed with his triumph and alarmed by Clinton's rapid advance toward Albany, Gates had accepted the terms of surrender dictated by Burgoyne without weighing their consequences. Washington was the first to spot the threatening loopholes.

> I am convinced that this event [Burgoyne's surrender] will not equal our expectation; and, that without great precaution, and very delicate management, we shall have all these men—if not the officers—opposed to use in the spring.

Congress was in a real dilemma. The terms of surrender had already been signed. To rescind the Convention, or even to alter it, would mean a breach of faith that would discredit this country in the eyes of all European nations. Burgoyne was already claiming violations of the agreement, but he was reckoning without the wily Witherspoon.

As a member of the committee appointed to sort out these confusing problems, he cut through to the heart of the matter. Let the Convention be ratified, he advised, let the prisoners of war be released, let Burgoyne have his way . . . BUT . . . and here was the master stroke:

> Resolved, therefore, that the embarkation of Lieutenant-General Burgoyne, and the troops under his command, be suspended until a distinct and explicit ratification of the Convention of Saratoga shall be properly notified by the Court of Great Britain to Congress.

Compliance with this demand would be a technical recognition of the Colonies as a free and independent nation—a condition the Crown would not possibly accept. But refusal would more than justify the retention of Burgoyne, his troops, and captured Hessian mercenaries on American soil.

The result of Witherspoon's inspired condition was that although Burgoyne was permitted to go home in early Spring, his troops were held as prisoners of war, and many hired Hessians were scattered throughout Pennsylvania and Virginia, where some of them took up permanent residence. They would never again take up arms against America.

Witherspoon served in Congress for a total of three and a half years. But he paid a dear price for the independence he had so vigorously supported. One son was killed in the Battle of Germantown and another taken prisoner by the British in 1781. After the war, he returned to the business of putting the College of New Jersey on a firm and solvent footing.

His powers of persuasion did not diminish with the passing years. At the age of sixty-eight, he persuaded the twenty-four-year-old widow of Dr. Armstrong Dill to marry him. An account of the ceremony performed by the President of Dickinson College and the ensuing celebration at Princeton appeared in the United States Gazette published in Philadelphia in June of 1791. It must, indeed, have been a memorable occasion:

> On Wednesday, after the President's return to Princeton with his amiable wife, a deputation of the students waited upon him to congratulate him upon the joyful occasion, and he politely gave them two days' holiday. In the evening, in regard to their worthy President, and to testify their joy on this happy marriage, the students illuminated the college, which afforded a grand and beautiful sight to the numerous spectators, who had assembled. There were six hundred candles in front of the college, which lighted almost instantly on signal given by the discharge of a canon, and on a like signal they were all immediately extinguished. During the illumination, a number of students in the belfry entertained the great concourse of people with a most agreeable and delightful concert of music from different kinds of instruments. The whole was conducted with elegance and taste. Joy sparkled in every eye, and every heart was glad.

The marriage between Ann Dill and John Witherspoon was happy but short-lived. Witherspoon, made the proud father of two children by his young wife, soon after lost his sight and died in 1794 at their home, Tusculum, outside Princeton. This free-thinking, freedom-loving, and persuasive patriot lies buried in the President's Lot at Princeton University.

NEW YORK

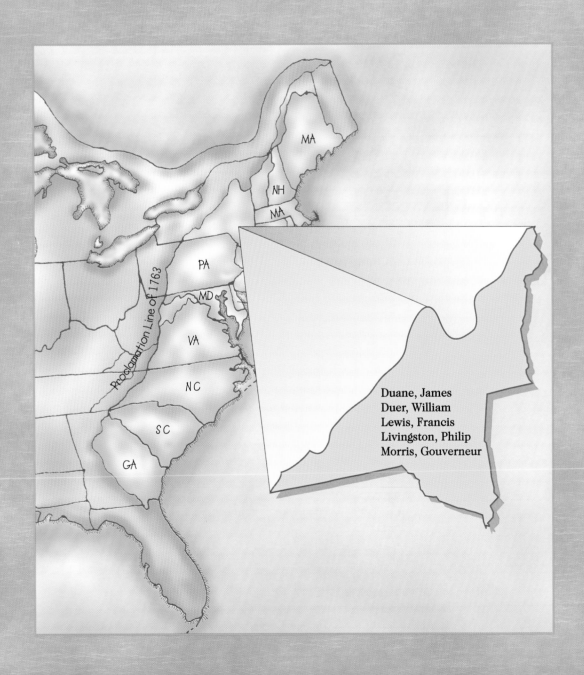

MA

NH

MA

PA

MD

VA

NC

SC

GA

Proclamation Line of 1763

Duane, James
Duer, William
Lewis, Francis
Livingston, Philip
Morris, Gouverneur

The Reluctant Revolutionist

JAMES DUANE

BIRTH: New York City
February 6, 1733

DEATH: Duanesburg, New York
February 1, 1797

COLONY: New York

EDUCATION: Private tutor

PROFESSION: Lawyer, Mayor of New York

AT YORK TOWN: September 30, 1777–
December 4, 1777

When James Duane was reading English Common Law in the office of James Alexander and was admitted to the Bar in 1754, he had no idea that, twenty years later, he would be working with men determined to free themselves of British rule and to establish a government of their own. Even in 1765, when many of his friends and colleagues were violently protesting the Stamp Act, he was protesting the protesters, attempting to suppress mob action. He was devoted to the English form of Government and held her laws in the highest respect. By the same token, he was also well aware of his rights as an Englishman, clearly understood that Parliament had infringed on them, but felt that such wrongs could only be redressed within the law . . . and by conciliation rather than by force.

When he was elected to the first Continental Congress, his position was clearly that of a conservative. But so compelling was his declaration of human rights, which appear in the Articles of Association, that two years later, it was incorporated, with some changes in phraseology, into the Declaration of Independence:

> Resolved: That they are entitled to life, liberty and property, and they have never ceded to any foreign power whatever, a right to dispose of either without their consent.

When Duane arrived in York Town in September of 1777, he had already been separated from his family for two years and five months. And, as he wrote to Governor Clinton, he was most reluctant to spend another winter without leave to visit them.

The long-awaited leave of absence was finally granted on December 3rd, but that very same day, Congress requested that he confer with the commissioners for Indian affairs in the Northern Department. Duane understood only too well the importance of the Indian problem. The neutrality of the Six Nations was of vital importance to the defense of both Pennsylvania and New York. Although the mighty Iroquois had agreed in principal to remain neutral, they had permitted each of the six tribes comprising the League to decide its own course of action. Only the Oneidas and Tuscaroras had elected to side with the Americans. Putting aside his personal reluctance to be away from his family, Duane served with the northern Indian commissioners until the spring of 1778, at considerable cost to himself and his loved ones, as described in a letter to Robert Morris dated March 19, 1778:

> I had the unhappiness, my dear Sir, on my return home, to find Mrs. Duane's health greatly impaired. The dangers and alarms to which she was exposed during the whole summer, joined to the fatigues and distress of a precipitate flight, and my unexpected long absence, were too violent for her fortitude and, in a manner, destroyed her whole nervous system. She recovers very slowly, and it requires all my care and attention to keep her in that flow of spirits which is absolutely necessary to give her any chance of health. Consider, my dear friend, what a drawback this is from the Happiness I proposed to myself in rejoining my family after so long an absence.

His distress was made even more acute by the knowledge that his sacrifice had been in vain. The Senecas and Cayugas, the two most powerful tribes, were in great sympathy with the Tory leader Colonel John Butler and the Butler Rangers, which threatened the New York frontier as well as the Wyoming Valley. Therefore, Washington's request for a party of the Oneidas and Tuscaroras to join the Grand Army had little hope of fulfillment.

James Duane continued to share in the up's and down's of the Continental Congress throughout its entire existence. He returned to New York City in 1783 and was chosen the first mayor under its new charter derived from the State legislature. He was also a member of the convention that adopted the Federal Constitution in 1788.

This New York delegate, who had been so reluctant to rebel against his motherland, gave unfailing loyalty and complete devotion to the new nation born of that rebellion. No stronger evidence of his regard for patriotic duty is to be found than in a letter to his beloved "Polly" (Mary Livingston Duane) written in 1781:

> I feel, my dearest Polly, the force of your observation, that although the State requires my assistance I have a tender and affectionate Wife and a young family who require my care. But what can I do? When called upon by the Voice of my Country, could I refuse, in a cause which my Conscience approved? No! An active part I MUST take—either in Council or in Field.

So ends the story of a "Reluctant Revolutionist" but an ever-willing and devoted patriot—James Duane.

A Man of Destiny

$\mathscr{W}$ILLIAM DUER

BIRTH: Devonshire, England
March 18, 1747

DEATH: New York City
April 18, 1799

COLONY: New York

EDUCATION: Eton

PROFESSION: Merchant, Financier

AT YORK TOWN: September 30, 1777–
November 8, 1777
November 1778–
January 1778
June 1, 1778–
June 27, 1778

By birth, education, and social position, William Duer had the makings of an English gentleman. His father, John Duer, was a wealthy owner of plantations in Antigua and Dominica. Young Duer followed a traditional British pattern—educated at a prestigious public school, then service in the army. He was then sent to India as aide-de-camp to Lord Robert Clive.

What dreams he may have had of a career in India were shattered by a severe attack of fever, which caused him to be sent home. After his father's death, Duer went to the West Indies to look after his property and to fulfill a Navy contract for masts and spars. But fate took him even farther from home. Armed with letters of introduction to prominent New Yorkers, he journeyed to America to purchase timber. On the advice of Philip Schuyler of Albany, he bought large tracts of land near Saratoga, built a sawmill, and became an American businessman.

By 1775, instead of supplying the British Navy with masts and spars, he was busy shipping planks for bridges ordered by the American army and outfitting American frigates. His zealous support of the rebel cause destined him to become a member of Congress. In 1777, along with Philip Schuyler, Philip Livingston, James Duane, and Gouverneur Morris, he was elected to represent the state of New York.

Although one of the youngest members (age twenty-eight), his ardor, eloquence, and boundless energy were such that, within two weeks, he was assigned to seven committees, the most important of which was his appointment to the Board of War.

Unfortunately, Congress was not what Duer had expected it would be. Shortly after his arrival, he wrote to John Jay:

> When I was sent here, I had some idea that I was entering into the Temple of Public Virtue. I am disappointed and chagrined.

From his position on the Board of War, Duer had first-hand knowledge of Washington's epic struggle at Valley Forge. He was outraged by the failure of Congress to supply flour, meat, and clothing to the suffering troops, and he was very much afraid that the army would revolt or desert to the enemy. He was also alarmed by the lack of wagons and horses to move artillery and baggage, as well as by lack of the proper care and maintenance of tents necessary for future campaigns. He voiced these concerns in no uncertain terms, charging the delegates with apathy, mismanagement, and downright stupidity.

Duer had planned to join Lafayette's expedition to Canada as a volunteer, only to discover that the Marquis had accused him of being a Tory sympathizer and an enemy of Washington. These allegations, however, do not hold up considering his reaction to the Conway Cabal. His absence because of illness had left New York without representation in Congress and put the anti-Washington faction in the majority. On hearing of the plotted, imminent disposal of the Commander-in-Chief, Duer was determined to return to block the vote. In defiance of his doctor's warning that such a move would be fatal, he ordered a litter to take him to York Town. Fortunately, before he could start on his journey, he received news that the scheme had been abandoned.

With the approach of spring, Duer became even more disgusted with Congress. He could not believe that so many delegates were leaving for home. On March 10th, he poured out his frustrations to his old friend and former delegate Robert Livingston:

> Common Sense must have convinced any but fools that betwixt the close of one campaign, and the opening of another, would be THE great period of Public Business; a number of Gentlemen acquainted with the business of Congress have returned to their homes, and left a few (and very few) men of business and real patriotism to struggle against men actuated by Contracte State Politicks, and rendered impenetrable to all the aspects of reason by the Superlative dint of Stupidity.

He also vainly appealed to both Gouverneur Morris and Robert Morris, imploring their immediate return, convinced that their joint leadership and talent for finance would bolster a shaky

Congress and improve a dangerous military situation. Or, as he put it:

> The joint exertions of some of us may save our Country and revive the expiring reputation of Congress. At least it is our Duty to try it.

And try he did, until he finished his term in 1779. In January of that year, after ensuring that his state was duly represented, he tendered his final resignation and turned his attention to happier affairs. The most important of these was his own wedding. In July, he married Kitty Alexander, daughter of the self-styled "Lord Stirling." The wedding was a storybook affair with a guest list of New York and New Jersey socialites. General George Washington himself gave the bride away.

By the end of the war, and through the early years of Washington's administration, William Duer became a wealthy and influential man, his feet seemingly planted on the road to a "happily-ever-after" life. But such was not to be the case.

Ironically, his business ventures and financial career followed a pattern similar to that of Robert Morris, whom he so much admired, both as a statesman and financial operator. Both Duer and Morris were, to some extent, victims of the age in which they lived—a period in which private businesses were growing bigger and bigger and were more and more dependent on the political climate. The basis of Duer's fortune was army contracts, but his bold—and often risky—enterprises included heavy investments in western and New England lands, which he and his partners hoped to sell on the European market.

Duer's enterprises were always carefully and skillfully planned, but according to one biographer, "his powers of execution were not equal to his conceptions. He undertook too much to give effective attention to detail" . . . and so most of his promotions failed.

By 1792, he was hopelessly insolvent, owed his creditors in excess of three million dollars, and was charged by the Federal government with irregularities in his accounts while serving six months as Assistant Secretary of the Treasury under Alexander Hamilton in 1789. His financial collapse was responsible for the first Panic of the Empire State.

Although no evidence of actual criminality was ever produced, he was sentenced to debtors' prison on March 23, 1792. Despite Hamilton's personal efforts to gain his release, Duer remained there until his death on May 7, 1799.

When judged by modern commercial morals, against a present-day background of political business involvement, it is hard to say whether this American patriot was a victim of his own bad judgment or merely a pawn in the hands of destiny.

FRANCIS LEWIS

BIRTH: Llandaff, Wales
March 21, 1713

DEATH: New York City
December 30, 1803

COLONY: New York

EDUCATION: Westminster School

OCCUPATION: Merchant

AT YORK TOWN: December 5, 1777–
June 27, 1778

The first part of the Francis Lewis story reads like an Horatio Alger success novel, but the latter portion bears the tragic overtones of an 18th-century King Lear. His father was the rector of Llandoff, in Glamorganshire, Wales. His mother, Amy Pettingall, was born within the shadow of Caernarvon Castle. Orphaned at an early age, the boy was reared by maternal relatives until he was admitted to Westminster School, from which he entered a mercantile house in London. When he was twenty-five years old, young Lewis sailed for the New World, not to seek but to build his fortune, a task for which he was well suited by intelligence and training,.

The business that he established in New York and Philadelphia involved European transactions, which took him back to England and to various foreign ports. His life as a merchant was not without adventure. Twice he was shipwrecked, and in 1756, he was captured by Indians. As a clothing contractor for British troops during the French and Indian War, he was present at the fall of Oswego and, together with other captives, was taken to Canada and later imprisoned in France until his release was arranged in 1763.

Meanwhile, his business had prospered, and by 1765, his name was well respected in New York financial circles. At fifty-two, he moved his wife, the former Elizabeth Annesly, and his family into a large, comfortable house in Whitestone, Long Island, where he settled down to enjoy the serenity of a well-earned retirement. By 1771, however, he was back in New York, paving the way for his eldest son's entry into the business world and renewing his commercial contacts on both sides of the Atlantic.

As the breach widened between the Colonies and Great Britain, there was never any doubt that Francis Lewis would stand with the patriots. He attended the Provincial Convention of 1774, was a member of the New York Revolutionary Committee, and served as a delegate to the Continental Congress from May of 1775 until November of 1779.

The year 1776 was a fateful year for the Lewis family. As a signer of the Declaration of Independence, the doughty New Yorker had become a target for British retaliation. Early in September, his Long Island home was completely destroyed by enemy troops, and his wife was taken prisoner. Although General Washington negotiated for her exchange some months later, Mrs. Lewis never recovered from the shock and hardships of her captivity, and she died in 1779.

In Congress, Lewis proved to be a tireless and conscientious worker, tackling the complexities of the Maritime, Secret, and Commercial Committees with the same care and tenacity that had distinguished his private business career. During the bleak winter at York Town, his confidence in Washington and ultimate victory remained unshaken. In a letter to Pierre Van Cortlant, Esq., President of the New York Senate, dated March 30, 1778, he wrote:

> If the public reports we have from abroad be true, we have nothing more to do than to exert ourselves this Campaign and our Independence will have a permanent establishment.

However, in November of the following year, broken in spirit by the untimely death of his wife, Lewis resigned from Congress and, with the exception of his post on the Admiralty Board, which he retained until 1781, withdrew from all public office.

The loss of his wife was not the only heartbreak that Francis Lewis had to bear. As he wrote to his daughter, Anne Robertson, in London:

> At the beginning of the Contest, I estimated myself worth twenty thousand pounds Currency, clear, and am now reduced to penury . . . and have not a son to turn to for advice or assistance, in so much that life has become a burden and the treatment I meet from your brothers, particularly from Morgan, will, I believe, soon put a period to it. Those of my acquaintances who caressed me in the Sunshine, now neglect me. Morgan's pride and arrogance is insufferable.

At the time of this pathetic disclosure, July 11, 1786, Lewis was living in a small house in the outskirts of New York City, having left his son's "Elegant Situation" in a last, brief gesture of independence. At seventy-three, he fully expected that "[a]ge would soon bring him the relief" he longed for, but such was not the case. For the next sixteen years, the lonely old man divided his time between the households of the two sons, whose treatment he described as such "would urge a Man of Stronger Nerves . . . to acts of despairation."

At the age of eighty-nine, this man who called himself "[a]n Affectionate but Afflicted Father," this patriot who had paid so dear a price for American independence, was laid to rest in an unmarked grave in New York's Trinity Churchyard.

PHILIP LIVINGSTON

BIRTH: Albany, N.Y.
January 15, 1716

DEATH: York Town, Pennsylvania
June 12,1778

COLONY: New York

EDUCATION: Yale

OCCUPATION: Merchant

AT YORK TOWN: May 5, 1778–
June 12, 1778

"A great, rough, rapid mortal" who "blustered away" from John Adams's verbal bombardments is hardly a well-rounded description of the extraordinary man who was Philip Livingston. Although Adams may have found it "impossible to hold a conversation with him," there were others who found him courteously receptive to their ideas, especially when those ideas concerned civic affairs and human welfare. "No one," observed the Royal Governor in 1755, "is more esteemed for energy, promptness, and public spirit than Philip Livingston."

Son of an aristocratic family, Philip Livingston was to the manor born. The princely style in which he was reared in Albany and his graduation from Yale in 1737 placed him among the social and academic elite. The fortune that he amassed from privateering during the French and Indian War and his astute ventures in the mercantile trade made him a financial baron. But basically, Livingston was a philanthropist rather than a financier. Although he and his wife, Christina TenBroeck, and their brood of nine children enjoyed the life of country gentry on their manorial estate at Brooklyn Heights, he had a unique concern for the less privileged.

This concern was manifest by his support of King's College (Columbia University), his efforts to organize the New York Library Association, and his donations to the New York Hospital in 1771. His philanthropy was uncommitted to any particular religious persuasion. He endowed a professorship of divinity at Puritan Yale, helped to build a meeting house for the first Methodist Society in America, and contributed generously to the city's first benevolent institution, the St. Andrew's Society.

Nor was Livingston himself totally committed to any particular political persuasion. He was a conservative, but not a conformist. As an opponent of the aristocratic ruling class, he was elected three times to the New York Assembly on the Whig ticket. His views on Britain's economic policy of 1764 were clearly expressed in an address to the Royal Governor, imploring his influence to obtain "that Great Badge of English Liberty, the right of his Majesty's subjects everywhere to be taxed only with their consent."

As conditions worsened, Livingston firmly supported the sober and dignified resistance of his peers, but he frowned on the riotous actions of the "Sons of Liberty," whom he considered to be extremists. He attended the Stamp Act Congress, strongly opposed the "Intolerable Acts," and from 1774 to 1778 represented his state in the Continental Congress.

But much as he believed in political and religious freedom, Livingston remained uncommitted to actual independence. He foresaw the long-term cost of disrupted trade relations with the Mother Country, and he also feared, as he told John Adams, that "[i]f England should turn us adrift, we should instantly go to civil war among ourselves."

During the Revolution, Livingston served in a dual capacity as a delegate to Congress and a member of the New York Legislature. He and his younger cousin Robert, a somewhat reluctant member of the committee to draft the Declaration of Independence, divided their time between these two bodies. Although absent from the actual voting on the Declaration, from which his state abstained, the elder statesman returned to Philadelphia in time to place his signature on the controversial document on August 2, 1776.

In the spring of 1778, having spent the winter as a New York Senator, Philip Livingston set out on what was to be his last journey. In response to Governor Clinton's urgent request that he return immediately to the Congress, in which the state was lacking its full quota of delegates, Livingston, then sixty-seven years old and suffering from dropsy, traveled on horseback from New York to York Town, a distance of well over two-hundred miles.

At his arrival on May 4th, Livingston found Congress in a jubilant mood, having that day ratified the long-awaited treaties with France, which promised financial and military aid to the flagging American cause. The following day, he quietly took his seat in Congress, but forty-eight hours later, his chair at the New York table was empty. Almost overnight, the "great, rough, rapid mortal" had become a very tired, very sick old man.

Despite the medical care of four fellow delegates—Doctors Josiah Bartlett, Oliver Wolcott, Jonathan Elmer, and Joseph Jones—Philip Livingston died at four o'clock in the morning of June 12, 1778, and was buried at sunset on the same day. His soldier son, Henry, summoned from his post at Valley Forge, described the scene at the German Reformed churchyard:

> The funeral was conducted in a manner suitable to his worth and station, being attended by all the military in town, the Congress, the strangers of distinction, and the most respectable citizens.

The inscription on his monument, later erected by his grandson, Stephen Van Renssalaer, describes him as "Eminently distinguished for his talents and rectitude." But his personal and private life, his selfless devotion to his country, and his dedication to the principles of humanity reveal him to have been endowed with an extra measure of greatness.

The Extra-Extra-Ordinary One

GOUVERNEUR MORRIS

BORN: Morrisania, New York
January 31, 1752

DIED: Morrisania, New York
November 6, 1816

COLONY: New York

EDUCATION: King's College (Columbia
University)

PROFESSION: Lawyer

AT YORK TOWN: January 20, 1778–
June 28, 1778

If Gouverneur Morris were living in today's world of tabloids and television, he would appear on every front page and every talk show in the country. His good looks, flamboyant lifestyle, wealth, social prestige, as well as his disregard of convention and his political position would make him an irresistible target for reporters and cameramen. Described by his biographers as a fop, a "Beau Brummel," and a "Ladies' Man," his romantic escapades were well known among the socially elite of two continents.

The product of wealthy, well-educated land-owners with strong mercantile interests, Morris was reared in a more or less frivolous society that did not equate pleasure with sin and guilt. He strictly adhered to what was considered a gentleman's personal code of honor, disdained excessive drinking and gaming, and thought that "women were wonderful creatures to whose pursuit a man could happily devote all the time he could spare from statecraft and finance."

What, then, did this light-hearted, pleasure-loving Don Juan have in common with men of such sober mien and moral rectitude as Adams, Witherspoon, Laurens and other delegates to Congress? The answer is . . . nothing . . . EXCEPT, a firm belief in a republican form of government and the American cause of liberty. Most of the older members found the flippancy and boldness of this twenty-five-year-old man of many foibles hard to take, but they did not hesitate to make full use of his brilliant mind, financial acumen, and powerful pen.

No sooner had he arrived at York Town than he was assigned to a committee concerning the military camp at Valley Forge, ostensibly "to regulate the army" but, as James Lovell more honestly expressed it, "to rap a Demi-God over the knuckles." However, if they counted on Morris to do the rapping, they were disappointed.

Morris was not one to bemoan misfortune, either his own or that of his country. "What is . . . is" was his philosophy. When things were not to his liking, he worked with might to change them. When his oldest half-brother inherited the fortune their father had amassed, Morris promptly set about the business of making one for himself. When at the age of twenty-eight he suffered the amputation of a leg, he wasted no time in lamentation but learned to function without it. He tackled the difficulties he encountered at Valley Forge with the same directness and objectivity that he employed in solving his personal problems.

He found George Washington at the lowest ebb of his career: being threatened by enemies in Congress and on the Board of War, his troops suffering from hunger and exposure, the army in a chaotic state of disorganization, and the entire war effort seriously threatened by lack of funds. Morris then picked up his pen as a weapon for change. He minced no words in placing the blame for the state of the troops squarely on Congress itself, and he exposed some of the under-handed dealings that were endangering his friend and army commander. He wrote directly to governors of individual states for supplies and strongly urged Congress to do the same. He recommended taxation as the only road to a firmer financial footing. He saw for himself the lack of discipline and military organization and pressed for the employment of Baron Von Steuben.

Morris remained at Valley Forge until mid-April, doing everything possible to strengthen Washington's position and to ameliorate the suffering of his men. Congress soon realized that "with the quill of a goose, a little ink, and the English language, he could do marvels in bringing the minds of men into unison." Consequently, Gouverneur Morris served on more committees, drafted more resolutions, and wrote more manifestos and important communiqués than any other man in Congress. It was his privilege and pleasure to be the author of *An Address to the American People,* setting forth the only possible peace terms that would be acceptable to the United States. This document, by order of Congress, was published across the nation and later, to his greatest satisfaction, was read before Parliament.

Never was a "house more divided against itself" than the Morris family. His half-brother, Lewis, was a Signer of the Declaration of Independence. Another half-brother, Richard, was in the service of his country; two sisters married staunch supporters of the Crown, and his mother, Sarah Gouverneur Morris, remained a Tory all her life. The following excerpt from a letter to his mother, headed "York Town, April 16, 1778," throws some light on his inner conflict and convictions:

> Whenever the present storm subsides, I shall rush with eagerness into the bosom of private life. But while it continues and while my Country calls for the exertions of that little share of abilities which it hath pleased God to bestow upon me, I hold it my indispensible Duty to give myself to her. I know that for such sentiments I am called a Rebel and that such sentiments are not fashionable among the folks you see. It is possible your maternal tenderness may lead you to wish that I would resign these sentiments. But that is impossible, and, therefore, for the present, I cannot see you.

After the war, his life became even more turbulent. Named Minister to France by President Washington in 1792, he lived in Paris during the Reign of Terror. His personal life took on all the aspects of intrigue, adventure, and romance that could constitute a novel. In 1799, he returned to Morrisania—"dear, quiet, happy home," he wrote in his diary. The final scenes of his life were played against a background of domesticity. On Christmas Day of 1809, he married the beautiful Ann Carey (Nancy) Randolph, to whom he proved to be the "best of husbands."

Few of today's visitors to St. Ann's Church in the Bronx realize that it stands on a portion of the original Morrisania Estate. The church and grounds were donated by their son, Gouverneur, in honor of his parents—and there they lie, side by side.

Only his name and the dates of his lifespan appear on the graveside marker of Gouverneur Morris. But so mixed were the elements in this complex man, so large the measure of his intelligence, energy, and emotion, as to justify the inscription: Of the great American statesmen, and patriots, he was the most extra-extra-ordinary of them all.

NORTH CAROLINA

Burke, Thomas
Harnett, Cornelius
Penn, John

Proclamation Line of 1763

The Great Objector

$\mathcal{T}$HOMAS BURKE

BIRTH: Galway, Ireland
1747

DEATH: Hillsboro, North Carolina
December 2, 1783

COLONY: North Carolina

EDUCATION: University (probably in Dublin)

PROFESSION: Lawyer

AT YORK TOWN: October 1, 1777–
October 13, 1777
March 12, 1778–
April 28, 1778

Had Thomas Burke not objected to anything and everything that hinted of oppression, he would not have espoused American independence, nor would the vehement expression of those objections have influenced North Carolina to be the first of the colonies to do the same. As a member of the committee to draft a state constitution, his radical objection to the conservative faction was responsible for the ideas of sovereignty of the people, separation of powers, separation of church and state, and annual elections being included.

Above all, Burke objected to incompetence. While at York Town in 1777, he convinced Congress to recommend the recall of General John Sullivan, whose incompetence he had witnessed at Brandywine. He also made sure that Sullivan was informed of the reason for his action. In a personal letter dated October 12, 1777, he told the General:

> I urged your recall with all the force I could, and thought it, and still do think it, necessary for the public good. My objection to you is want of sufficient talent and I consider it as your misfortune, not fault. It is my duty as far as I can, to prevent it being the misfortune of my country.

Washington, however, refused to act on the recommendation for recall, because he did not wish to set a precedent for punishment of defeat.

Burke also objected to the Articles of Confederation, especially to Article 11, which allowed

97

Canada to join the colonies in revolution if it, too, chose to adopt this legislation. At his insistence, that article was almost entirely rewritten. Although he was not present for the completion of the Articles, he continued to oppose them, article by article, when they were submitted to the North Carolina Assembly of which he was a member. The result was that North Carolina did not ratify the Articles in their entirety until April 24, 1778.

As might be expected, Burke's quick temper and forthright speech did not make him the most popular of delegates. He was especially unpopular with Eliphalet Dyer of Connecticut, who expressed himself freely on the subject in the postscript to a letter to William Williams:

> P.S. The Disturber, I Mean B--ke, has just come after inducing Nth C-----na to dissent from Confederation (Or) a great part of it, is now in Congress to the universal sorrow of every member.

The incident arose over the drafting of a letter to Washington intended to assuage his resentment of a previous communiqué on the matter of an exchange of prisoners with the British. The current draft had been debated all day—deleting, changing, rewriting, rephrasing—until Burke, with a splitting headache and his ears ringing with the strident voices of argument, felt his temper boiling over. After voting in the affirmative on a paragraph that had been argued all afternoon, he declared that the states might vote as they liked but that he was going to "adjourn himself." Thereupon, he stalked out of the room, followed by Edward Langworthy of Georgia, leaving Congress without a quorum to conclude their business.

Burke and Langworthy had no sooner reached their lodgings than a messenger arrived with a summons for their immediate return. Langworthy politely complied, but not Burke, who replied "the Devil take him if he would come," it was too late (after 10 PM) and too unreasonable. The next day, Congress called for an explanation of his behavior. Burke was totally unrepentant, refusing to apologize for anything he had said or done and claiming that he was responsible solely to his state. He was given until Monday, April 12th, to prepare a defense.

The defense that Burke prepared in writing was unacceptable to Congress, which apparently did not bother him at all, given the conviction he expressed in his final paragraph: "I do not mean to submit myself to any jurisdiction but that of the State I represent." Accordingly, he left York Town on April 19th to lay his case before the Assembly of North Carolina, where he was not only vindicated but also re-elected to Congress. He continued to serve until 1779, when he was elected governor of that state.

So energetic was he in recruiting soldiers and assembling supplies against the British invasion in 1781 that he was captured during a special raid on Hillsboro and held in close confinement on Sullivan's Island. He was finally paroled to James Island, where he received better treatment, but he managed to escape to the headquarters of General Greene. He eventually returned to North Carolina, but his health had been so seriously affected by imprisonment and overwork that he died in 1783 at the age of thirty-six. The life of this fiery patriot was a testament to his political creed "that undue or unreasonable exercise of any power, though lawful power, is Tyrannical and that no free man is bound to submit to it."

The Man Who Wanted To Go Home

CORNELIUS HARNETT

BIRTH: Chowan County, North Carolina
    April 20, 1723

DEATH: Wilmington, North Carolina
    April 20, 1781

COLONY: North Carolina

EDUCATION: Self-taught (letters, music)

PROFESSION: Planter, Merchant

AT YORK TOWN: September 30, 1777–
    April 1778

During the nine months that Congress met in York Town, the malady of homesickness reached epidemic proportions among the members, but no case on record was as severe as that suffered by Cornelius Harnett. He not only missed his wife and loved ones, he longed for all the sights, sounds, comforts, smells, and tastes of home.

Home to Harnett was Wilmington and the Cape Fear region of North Carolina, where he first became involved in the struggle against British encroachment of American rights. So vigorous and effective were his actions in opposing taxes on sugar, stamps, and tea, as well as against the hated Townshend Acts, that he won the supreme accolade of American patriots—he was dubbed the "Sam Adams of North Carolina" by John Quincy of Massachusetts. In 1776, as President of the Committee of Safety, Harnett acted, virtually, as Governor of North Carolina, the first executive officer not appointed by the Crown. As such, he was chosen to read the Declaration of Independence to the crowd assembled in front of the Halifax County Court House, after which he was carried through the streets by the excited mob, all swearing allegiance to a free and independent nation.

All these years of service necessitated frequent absences from home, but none were so protracted and taxing as his four terms in the Continental Congress. At the beginning of his stay in York Town, the main business before the House was completion of the Articles of Confederation, a subject close to his heart. He had long decried the existing hostility among the colonies, and he realized the importance of unity over sovereignty. So, he listened patiently to the long arguments, the angry voices, and the table-thumpings with which they were finally hammered into shape. Upon their completion, he wrote to his colleague Thomas Burke:

> The Child Congress has been big with these two years past is, at last, brought forth. I fear it will by several Legislators be thought a little deformed (you will think it a monster) but I believe our Affairs must be ruined without it.

His strong support of unity did not diminish his concern for his home state. He fought valiantly against disproportionate taxation, disregard for equipment, lack of recognition of her troops, and lack of coastal defenses. As fall darkened into winter, his correspondence, both personal and official, reflected more and more frustration with his job, calling it "the most disagreeable and troublesome office."

To add to his miseries, he also fell victim to the torment of gout:

> I have lately had one of the severest fitts of the Gout I ever had in my life. I have been confined to my room these five weeks, unable to help myself, having it in both feet, one knee, and my right hand and arm. It is with great pain that I am able to hold a pen in my hand this day.

It was necessary, pain or no pain, that he should keep the Governor up to date on the progress of the war. In the absence of a newspaper, he was forced to make these reports by letter. When he was well enough to attend to his duties, he suffered from extreme fatigue: "I never in my life went through so much fatigue, being obliged to sit all day in Congress, and often, very often, in the Treasury Board till eleven at night."

Meanwhile, his personal treasury was under a severe strain, as his living expenses far exceeded his salary. He warned Congress that inflation posed a much greater danger to the country than the British armed forces. Furthermore, he was convinced that nowhere was it so bad as in the very state where they were meeting. In fact, he considered not just York Town but the whole of Pennsylvania to be "the most inhospitable scandalous place I ever was in."

By Christmas, the worst possible season for homesickness, Harnett was at his lowest ebb. In a message to his wife, requesting two or three gallons of pickled oysters and a dozen or more dried fish, he included the comment that "even if they stank, they would be pleasing," indicating, at least to some extent, the depths of his misery. In general, however, he did not want his wife to know either the state of his health nor the extent of his discomfort, but to his friend and business partner William Wilkinson, he suffered no such inhibitions. In a letter dated December 28, 1777, he wrote:

> If I once more return to my family, all the Devils in Hell shall not separate us. The honor of being once a Member of Congress is sufficient for me. I acknowledge it is the highest honor a free state can bestow on its members. I shall be careful to ask for nothing more, but will sit down under my own Vine and Fig Tree* (for I have them both at Poplar Grove) where none shall make me afraid except for the boats of the British Cruisers. I wish you the Compliments of the season.

It would not have been surprising had this bone-weary, pain-wracked man, heartsick and alone—abandoned even by his body servant—would have simply packed up and left. But the thought of leaving his home state without representation in Congress, apparently never crossed his mind. Having completed his term of service, Harnett finally left York Town on April 22nd for Maynard (later Hilton), his beautiful estate in Wilmington, where by a cruel twist of fate he was not permitted to live "happily ever after."

Only eight months later, the British occupation of the Cape Fear area made him the prize target of the enemy. Harnett had been entrusted with a large sum of money for the purchase of supplies, so that he was forced to leave his home safely in advance of the British troops. But a sudden and severe attack of gout made it impossible to proceed any further than the home of a friend, James Spicer, where acting on a Tory tip Major James Craig arrested him. Unable to walk or ride, he was thrown "like a sack of meal" across the back of a horse and taken to Wilmington. There he was held prisoner in a roofless block house, where he died several months later from exposure.

The gravestone of Cornelius Harnett, at St. James Church in Wilmington, North Carolina, bears a quotation from Alexander Pope, but a more suitable line may have been taken from the epitaph of the 19th-century poet Robert Louis Stevenson:

> This be the verse you grave for me
> Here he lies where he longed to be.

Forever a part of his beloved North Carolina soil.

---

* A reference from the *Book of Micah,* Chapter 4, Verse 4.

The Eloquent Country Lawyer

JOHN PENN

BIRTH: Caroline County, Virginia
    May 17, 1741

DEATH: Williamsboro, Granville County,
    North Carolina
    September 14, 1788

COLONY: North Carolina

EDUCATION: Self-taught

PROFESSION: Lawyer

AT YORK TOWN: September 30, 1777–
    March 18, 1778

Eloquent is the word that best describes John Penn. Even Sam Ervin, the self-styled country lawyer of Watergate fame, might easily have succumbed to the eloquence of this 18th-century country lawyer.

John Penn's father, Moses Penn, was a man with the money—but not the inclination—to provide his son with an education worthy of his intelligence. So, the boy had to be content with the meager educational opportunities offered by the common schools of Caroline County. At the age of eighteen, however, after the death of his father, young Penn began the study of law with a distant relative, the distinguished Edmund Pendleton. So rapid was his progress that within three years he was admitted to the Bar. In 1744, he left his successful law practice and moved his wife and three children to Granville County, North Carolina, where he soon earned an even greater reputation as an able and competent attorney.

From the very beginning of his career, Penn displayed a real talent for oratory. His style was neither flamboyant nor bombastic but, rather, a gentle, low-key, irresistibly moving eloquence. His opponents, more often than not, found themselves yielding to the "sweet voice of reason."

His eminence as a lawyer, his political convictions, and his personal record of public service qualified him for election to the Provincial Assembly. Only a few weeks later, he was sent to the Continental Congress. There, in accordance with instructions from his state and the dictates of his own conscience, he signed the Declaration of Independence.

He arrived in York Town with his colleague, the homesick Cornelius Harnett, and the rest of the men in flight from Philadelphia in September of 1777 and served there until the following March. The same qualities that made him a popular choice for Congress, especially his efficiency and discretion, won him many friends in that body. The majority shared the opinion of Cornelius Harnett, as expressed to Governor Caswell: "His conduct as a Delegate and a Gentleman has been worthy and disinterested" (i.e., without self-interest).

Penn's correspondence from York Town bears evidence of the same quiet reasoning and factual accuracy that characterized his oratory. An example of his powers of persuasion is to be found in a personal altercation with Henry Laurens, which took place in Philadelphia in 1779. Laurens and Penn were on opposite sides of accusations against Robert Morris regarding the mishandling of accounts for the Secret Committee (Department of Commerce). Penn had defended Morris in the affair, which had begun eight months earlier at York Town. As an outgrowth of this official disagreement, a personal quarrel erupted between the two men. Laurens, on some real or imaginary point of honor, challenged Penn to a duel—which Penn accepted. However, on their way to the dueling ground, Penn persuaded Laurens to bury the hatchet, to forget their differences, and the whole matter was dropped.

John Penn served in Congress for five years before returning to his home at Stovall, North Carolina. He responded to the Governor's call for help when General Cornwallis threatened to invade the western part of the state and was given dictatorial powers in its defense—truly a mark of public confidence.

Aside from serving a brief stint as State Tax Receiver, Penn completely retired from public service to live out the remainder of his forty-seven years in the role he most enjoyed—that of a country lawyer. At his death in 1778, he was buried in the family graveyard beside his wife, Susan. But in 1894 his body was moved to Guilford Courthouse National Military Park in Greensboro, North Carolina, where it remains beside the grave of William Hooper. The monument, a twenty-foot-tall statue of an orator bearing a scroll, is inscribed as follows:

IN MEMORIAM
WILLIAM HOOPER AND JOHN PENN
Delegates from North Carolina 1776 to the Continental Congress and Signers of the Declaration of Independence. Their remains were reinterred here 1894, [Joseph] Hewes grave is lost. He was the third Signer.

PENNSYLVANIA

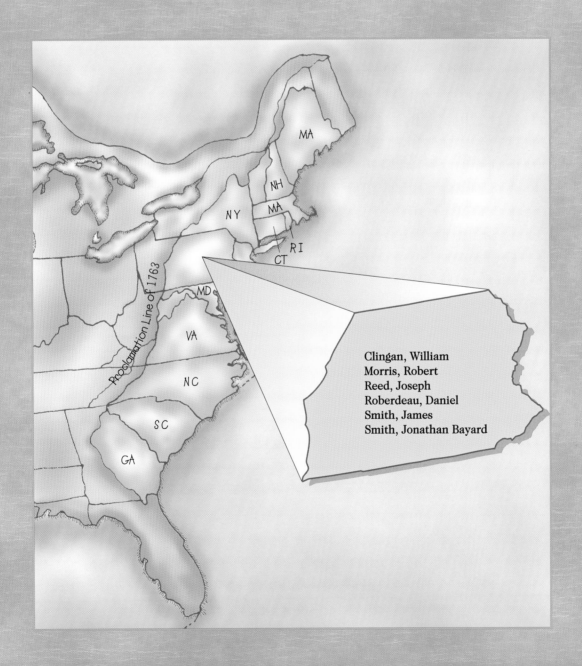

Proclamation Line of 1763

MA
NH
MA
NY
RI
CT
MD
VA
NC
SC
GA

Clingan, William
Morris, Robert
Reed, Joseph
Roberdeau, Daniel
Smith, James
Smith, Jonathan Bayard

A Forgotten Character

WILLIAM CLINGAN

BIRTH: Wagontown, Chester County
(Date unknown)

DEATH: May 9, 1790

COLONY: Pennsylvania

EDUCATION: Common School; largely
self-taught

OCCUPATION: Lawyer

AT YORK TOWN: November 1, 1777–
March 24, 1778
April 25, 1778–
May 19,1778

History, like all forms of human drama, has always had a large number of minor characters in its cast—participants whose roles, while not important of themselves, support the leading characters. Such a player was William Clingan, whose brief appearance on the congressional stage supported the leading men and advanced the plot of the great drama of American Independence.

Although elected to Congress in September of 1777, Clingan did not make his entrance until November 1st, in time to participate in the final drafting of the Articles of Confederation and to vote on their ultimate adoption. Perhaps his delay was, in part, due to his own property having been ravaged by the enemy in the Brandywine actions.

As a private citizen, William Clingan was a man of sterling character, a solid Pennsylvania patriot, well liked by his neighbors and highly respected as the magistrate of West Caln Township in Chester County. His public popularity is evidenced by successive appointments to the office of Justice of the Peace from 1757 to 1786. He also served as President Judge of the Chester County courts between 1780 and 1786.

Clingan's political convictions and revolutionary sentiments reflected those of his fellow citizens in the area. The intensity of those feelings was dramatically illustrated at the wedding of his nephew and namesake, William Clingan, Jr., on June 17, 1778. According to the story, every male guest in attendance had been in military service. After the ceremony, it was agreed by all present that the unmarried ladies would form an organization called "The Whig Association of the Unmarried Ladies of America." Their pledge was never to give their hand in marriage to any gentleman who had not first proved himself as a devoted patriot by turning out when called to the service of his country. The young women thus ensured themselves against ever becoming mothers of "a race of slaves and cowards!"

The only surviving official communiqué bearing Clingan's signature is a congressional report on the case of the imprisoned Rev. Batwell, the Anglican Rector who had refused to eliminate prayers for the Royal Family demanded by Holy Orders. Batwell had petitioned Congress for parole on the grounds of ill health. Although Congress did not make its final decision until December 27th, this progress report was addressed to Thomas Wharton, Esq., President of the Commonwealth of Pennsylvania, on November 13th, 1777.

After the war, Clingan resumed his quiet life in a large stone farmhouse on Old Lancaster Road near his birthplace. During his career, he was said to have amassed a modest fortune, no doubt considerably over-valued by neighbors. Rumors of a large sum of money in gold coin reached the ears of a notorious band of robbers known as the Doanes, inspiring them to burglarize his home. When they came upon a heavy bag giving forth a reassuring clink, they made off with it. One of the robbers, later executed, described to Clingan, when he visited the man in prison, their chagrin when they discovered the bag contained the pennies from the Sunday School collection awaiting bank deposit.

Clingan's long and rather under-recorded life ended in 1790. His body lies in the Upper Octorara Burial Ground, Chester County. If it were possible for the entire cast of Continental Congress to assemble for a final curtain call, William Clingan would take his bow with all the others, acknowledging the applause of an appreciative audience—a grateful nation.

Rich Man–Poor Man

ROBERT MORRIS

BORN: Liverpool, England
January 31, 1734

DIED: Philadelphia, Pennsylvania
May 8, 1806

COLONY: Pennsylvania

EDUCATION: Philadelphia tutor

PROFESSION: Merchant, Banker, Financier

AT YORK TOWN: September 1777–
December 12, 1777
May 13, 1778–
May 15, 1778

How did a country, virtually bankrupt and practically without credit, manage to conduct eight years of warfare that ended with the defeat of a nation as rich and powerful as Great Britain? This question remained a puzzle to the British, because they did not realize the power of America's "Secret Weapons"—Washington in the field, Franklin in Paris, and Robert Morris in Philadelphia.

Robert Morris, acknowledged Financier of the Revolution, first set foot on American soil at the age of thirteen, when he joined his father, a tobacco exporter, in Oxford, Maryland. With only a meager schooling in Philadelphia, Morris went to work for the prestigious shipping firm of Thomas and Charles Willing. Seven years later, he became a partner in the firm and a member of the Board of Directors.

As a merchant, he naturally protested the Stamp Act, but he did not, to any extent, participate in any other anti-British activities. In 1775, after Concord and Lexington, Congress contracted with his firm for arms and ammunition, so it was in the line of business that he found himself to be a member of the Pennsylvania Council of Safety, the Committee of Correspondence, the Provincial Assembly, the State Legislature, and in 1776, the Continental Congress.

By July 1, 1776, Robert Morris was one of the wealthiest men in the colonies and an influential resident of Philadelphia, where he lived with his charming and socially prominent wife, Mary White, sister of the esteemed rector of Christ Church. On the fateful issue of that day, however, Morris maintained a position of caution. Although in favor of independence, he felt that the actual Declaration was premature—and so voted against it. However, in order not to split the Pennsylvania vote, he purposely absented himself from Congress the next day, with the result that Pennsylvania was recorded in the affirmative. His name also appears among the signatures on that most treasured document.

Of the delegates at York Town, Robert Morris is the only one who could have been called a "commuter." He moved his wife and seven children to Manheim, twenty miles away, living there with them and traveling back and forth as necessary.

From the start, Congress had the good sense to put Morris in charge of the Finance Department and the procurement of supplies. At his own expense, he contributed thousands of barrels of flour to Washington's starving troops, pressured the states to raise money, borrowed on his own personal credit, slashed all government and military expenses, and tightened accounting procedures. It was Morris who loaned ten-thousand dollars to pay the men who participated in the surprise attack and capture of Trenton, and it was Morris who financed Washington's Yorktowne campaign, which ended with the surrender of Cornwallis.

Meanwhile, his personal fortune was flourishing—so much so, in fact, that he was charged with profiteering! After an investigation, he was completely exonerated. But, because of the common conviction that where there's smoke, there must be some fire, his reputation was tarnished.

In 1781, he was made Superintendent of Finance, with unlimited powers. In that same year, when the government was more than two-million dollars in debt, he organized the Bank of North America, which restored public confidence in a currency that was practically worthless. The bank was also able to loan four-hundred-thousand dollars to the stricken nation.

Morris was a member of the Constitutional Convention of 1787. As first President of the United States, Washington offered him the position of Secretary of the Treasury, but he declined, recommending Alexander Hamilton in his stead.

It seems incredible that a financial wizard who once arranged loans totalling one-million, four-hundred-thousand dollars to his country should have sunk into abject poverty in little more than a decade, but such was the case. Morris invested heavily—and unsuccessfully—in upper New York and western lands. By 1778, he had lost everything—his fortune, his home, his estate in what is now Fairmount Park, and an incomplete palatial mansion on Chestnut Street designed by Pierre L'Enfant. He had also caused the financial ruin of one-hundred-fifty investors, sixty-seven of whom he is said to have owed at least thirty-million dollars. Although he was not mistreated during the three years of his confinement in debtors' prison, his health was undermined, and his spirit was broken.

The only two men of national importance who paid any attention to his plight were President Washington, for whom he had done so much, and his old friend and business associate Gouverneur Morris. Washington dined with him in prison, and Morris visited him as often as possible, showing real compassion for his situation. On his release in 1802, Gouverneur Morris took him to his home for a short period of recuperation, as described in his diary: "He came to me, lean, low-spirited, and [penniless]. I sent him home fat, sleek, in good spirits and the means of living comfortably the rest of his life. So much for the air of Morrisania." It was the generous annuity of fifteen-thousand dollars, set up in his wife's name by his good friend, that saw him through the last four years of his life.

Robert Morris died in 1806. His gravesite in the yard of Christ Church, his statue in front of the Old Custom House, and a plaque marking the location of our oldest banking institution, the Bank of North America, are Philadelphia's only visible reminders of this man. He is best remembered in the pledge he made to a desperate and bankrupt Congress in 1781: "The United States may command everything I have . . . except my integrity." These words were spoken by a man who John Adams described as a "master of understanding and an honest heart."

Washington's Aide-de-Camp

JOSEPH REED

BIRTH: Trenton, New Jersey
August 27, 1741

DEATH: Philadelphia, Pennsylvania
March 5, 1785

COLONY: Pennsylvania

EDUCATION: Philadelphia Academy,
College of New Jersey
(Princeton University)
Middle Temple, London

PROFESSION: Lawyer, Statesman

AT YORK TOWN: April 6, 1778–
April 11, 1778

We can only wonder about the effect that an eloquent, powerful force such as Joseph Reed would have made on Congress and the shaping of the Articles of Confederation had he been elected as a delegate earlier. Reed's services, however, were destined to be employed elsewhere—and quite often—by George Washington's side.

Joseph Reed's family took up residence in Philadelphia when he was still an infant. Like many in his family's circumstances, he received an early, classically based education and was sent to Princeton for "finishing." But more was in store for Reed's promising mind. He next studied law, then journeyed to London to hone his legal skills at the prestigious Middle Temple. The controversies that swirled around the implementation of the Stamp Act precipitated his return to America, where he opened what became a most promising law practice.

Reed had made important connections while in London, not the least of which was with Esther DeBerdt, for whom he returned to England to retrieve as his bride in 1770. Her family's connections gained him an interesting position, and one that, in part, helped to prepare him for his later role as Washington's secretary—he was appointed by the British Colonial Office to keep them informed of the state of the colonies as the movement for independence was gaining momentum. This he did between December, 1773 and February, 1775, which caused some patriots to question his loyalties. He attempted to make his own position clear in his last communication on February 10th, when he stated, "This country will be deluged in blood before it will submit to any other taxation than by their own legislature."

Joseph Reed entered into the role of patriot with enthusiasm. He served as a member of Pennsylvania's Committee of Correspondence and was also made president of the Pennsylvania Convention.

On George Washington's arrival in Boston during the summer of 1775, Reed was offered the job of the new Commander-in-Chief's aide-de-camp. As an astute lawyer and a ready writer, he was the right person for the job. There can be no doubt that the opening of the army's books of record, the preparing of forms, the directing of correspondence, the composing of legal and state papers, and the establishment of general rules and etiquette of headquarters can be traced to Joseph Reed.

In January, 1776, Reed was appointed the army's Adjutant General, and he played an active role in that year's campaigning. Following the Battle of Long Island, the British wished to open negotiations to encourage Washington to surrender. Then a colonel, Reed, under a flag of truce, represented Washington's interests. The British communication was simply addressed to "George Washington, Esquire." Immediately recognizing the snub, Reed declined to receive it.

In 1777, Joseph Reed was appointed Brigadier General. Shortly thereafter, he was offered command of all Continental cavalry and was also appointed Pennsylvania's first Chief Justice. Both these honors he declined, preferring to remain in the field as a volunteer aide. Because of his student days at Princeton and his familiarity with the area, he provided critical service throughout the New Jersey campaign. Often in the thick of things, Reed had horses shot out from under him in three separate engagements.

Reed was elected to the Continental Congress in 1777, but again, he chose to remain with Washington in the field. In 1778, he finally joined that body in time to sign the Articles of Confederation. While a delegate, Joseph Reed, along with Henry Laurens, Francis Dana, and Robert Morris, were secretly approached by the British commissioners, newly arrived in America, to discuss terms of peace. Reed was offered ten-thousand pounds Sterling and "the most valuable office in the colonies" if he would use his considerable influence to "promote a reconciliation." His reply clearly demonstrated his full measure as an American patriot of the first order:

> I am not worth purchasing; but such as I am, the King of Great Britain is not rich enough to do it.

Also in 1778, Reed was elected president of the Supreme Executive Council of Pennsylvania, and he held that position for three years. He continued to serve the army from outside its ranks and, by using his good will and influences, helped to quell the insurrection of the Pennsylvania Line in 1781. Earlier, he had served the Commander-in-Chief by being one of the first to recognize the traitorous activities of Benedict Arnold.

Joseph Reed later returned to his law career. He also served as a trustee for the founding of the University of Pennsylvania. In political matters, he favored both the gradual abolition of slavery and the reduction of the proprietary powers of William Penn's heirs. In 1784, in failing health, he returned to England for three months. The sea voyages did him little good, for the following year, he died at forty-three years of age. Reed was described as one who:

> displayed inflexible patriotism, boldness, and a comprehensive mind in his public career, wielding a vast influence in council and field. In private life he was known to be purely moral, and a faithful friend.

Indeed, he was a friend and aide-de-camp to George Washington in times and places when friendship and patriotism were needed most.

Fort Roberdeau

A Generous General

DANIEL ROBERDEAU

BIRTH: St. Christopher, West Indies
     1727

DEATH: Winchester, Virginia
     January 5, 1795

COLONY: Pennsylvania

EDUCATION: Business

PROFESSION: Merchant

AT YORK TOWN: September 30, 1777–
     May 31, 1778

General Daniel Roberdeau was the only delegate to the Continental Congress who opened his heart, his home, and his purse strings to the American cause of independence. An extremely concise but accurate biography of this Pennsylvania patriot is to be found in a letter from John Adams to Abigail Adams dated October 9, 1777:

> My dearest Friend: I told you in a former letter that I lodged at General Roberdeau's. This Gentleman is of French extraction, his Father was a rich Planter of the Island of St. Christopher where my Friend was born and where he has or had an estate. He has large Property in England, in Virginia, in Philadelphia, in York Town, and in various other parts of Pennsylvania. He also has large property in our American Funds, has put great sums into the Loan Office.
>
> His wife was a daughter of Mr. Bostwick of New York, a famous minister, sister to Mrs. McDougall, the Lady of General McDougall, two as fine women as American ever produced, excepting one! Mrs. Roberdeau was a beauty. A fine figure—good taste—great sense—much knowledge—a fine temper. But she is no more.
>
> The General's two sisters keep his house—the one, a widow, Mrs. Clymer who has a son—the other, a maiden Lady, Miss Elizabeth Roberdeau.

Roberdeau opened his heart to the American cause almost as soon as the war began, when he

111

was elected Colonel of the Second Battalion of "Associators," which was formed as a body for home defense during the French and Spanish War. On July 4, 1776, he was made Brigadier General of the Pennsylvania Troops, as the Associators were then called.

When in 1777 he was elected to Congress and came to York Town, he rented a house on South George Street, just a stone's throw away from the Court House, and moved his family into it. Although it was a spacious, two-and-a-half-story dwelling, one of the larger in town, he opened his home to five of his fellow delegates, and it was soon filled to over-flowing. Although the quarters were cramped, the guests enjoyed a warmth and comfort not to be found elsewhere.

The generous general first opened his purse to this country when one of his privateers captured a prize vessel. His own portion of the winnings, twenty-two dollars in silver, he immediately donated to Congress. His generosity persisted throughout the war years. In April of 1778, he took a leave from Congress "because of a serious shortage of lead for ammunition" to work a lead mine near Bedford, Pennsylvania. Not only was the mine on his personal property, he also personally defrayed the expense of building a fort for protection against Indian raids while the work was in progress.

Nothing grieved and angered this kind-hearted man so much as the frustration and suffering of Washington and his army at Valley Forge. Much of his correspondence with Thomas Wharton, President of the Executive Council of Pennsylvania, which was then meeting in Lancaster, reflects his disgust that such privation should exist in the midst of plenty.

When a cold, blustery autumn presaged a long, severe winter, the shortage of shoes was Roberdeau's immediate concern. Surely, as he pointed out to Wharton, our own troops should not go barefoot when our worst enemies were abundantly supplied. That Lancaster was in possession of the largest stores of leather on record did nothing to allay Roberdeau's indignation.

As the winter worsened, so did the condition of the army. In January, when Washington was under pressure to attempt the recapture of Philadelphia and being harshly criticized for not doing so, Roberdeau became even more impassioned:

> I could weep over my suffering country, cramped at this season for vigorous exertion, by want of provision with which our country abounds . . . tears of blood have been shed for the opportunities lost through want of Provisions . . . for the Lord's sake, let us exert every nerve to save our country, which must now be done by immediate supplies from this State.

In modern parlance, this open-handed, outspoken patriot "put his money where his mouth was" and lived to see the preservation of the land he held so dear. For some years after the war, Daniel Roberdeau resided in Alexandria, Virginia, where he frequently entertained George Washington, to whom his loyalty had never faltered.

$\mathcal{J}$AMES SMITH

BIRTH: Dublin, Ireland
c. 1719–1720

DEATH: York, Pennsylvania
July 11, 1806

COLONY: Pennsylvania

EDUCATION: Rev. Alison's Academy,
New London, Pennsylvania
Philadelphia Academy

PROFESSION: Lawyer

AT YORK TOWN: December 16, 1777 until
Adjournment
(Resided in York 1750
until his death)

During the summer of 1773, young Alexander Graydon arrived in York Town to study law with the county's first resident attorney, Samuel Johnston. His journal reflects how different he found life on the frontier compared with the social arena of Philadelphia. This young man's journal also provides an interesting description of York Town's own congressional delegate, James Smith. Graydon described him as "an oddity":

> This was Mr. James Smith, the lawyer, then in considerable practice. He was probably between forty and fifty years of age, fond of his bottle and young company, and possessed of an original species of drollery. This consisted more in the manner than in the matter for which reason it is scarcely possible to convey a just notion of it to the reader. In him it much depended on the uncouthness of gesture, a certain ludicrous cast of countenance, and a drawling more of utterance, which taken in conjunction with his eccentric ideas, produced an effect, irresistibly comical. The most trivial incident from his mouth was stamped with his originality, and in relating one evening how he had been disturbed in his office by a cow, he gave inconceivable zest to his narrative by telling how she thrust her nose into the door and there did roar like a Numidian Lion.

As droll and comic a figure as James Smith surely was, he was also possessed of a keen mind for law and business and the heart of a patriot.

Smith was born in Ireland, although when is a mystery, for he would never tell his age. His family moved to Pennsylvania in 1727. After his classical schooling, he moved to Lancaster to study law, then he moved west to the frontier, where he learned the art of surveying from Thomas Cookson, who had laid out York Town's lots in 1741. Settling in Shippensburg, Smith set up a legal practice; following a few years of success, he resettled in York Town.

By 1771, James Smith was a well-known figure to those who lived west of the Susquehanna River. He had also acquired an iron forge and furnace— Codorus Furnace, the ruins of which still stand north of York—as well as substantial farmland throughout the county. It was during that time that he also developed a substantial taste for the idea of independence. Smith played an initial role in the recruitment and training of a local militia as early as 1773. He was a delegate to the provisional conference in Philadelphia, and he served as a delegate to the State convention in January of 1775. Locally, he was the chair of York Town's Committee of Safety.

As news of the fighting at Bunker Hill and Breeds Hill around Boston spread through the colonies, a call arose for Continental reinforcements. A company of York Town riflemen, under the command of Captain Michael Doudel and, in part, trained by James Smith, was among the first to respond to the request. Smith became active in the formal organization of the militia and was commissioned a Colonel. He played a key role in establishing the "Flying Camp" in 1776, and that year, he was also elected a delegate to the Continental Congress, where he signed the Declaration of Independence.

But James Smith's jovial side never left him, as a letter to his wife dated August 15, 1776, attests:

> I am glad however I did not write yesterday morning as I intended being then in a bad humor, having lost a New Cane at a Turtle Feast with Mr. Hancock and ye Delegates last Week, and my New Hat and 37 dollars in Paper money all which I got safe yesterday. I got my Cane at ye New Tavern. Genl. Worster had taken my hat in a Mistake and the Negro woman found ye money in my bed room amongst some old Papers

Smith went on to describe a flare up of "ye Rheumatism" brought on by sleeping with open windows and how various cures had been suggested to him, including one by John Hancock:

> Mr. Hancock is a better Doctor, as he has something of ye Gout himself and has promised me some Pine buds to make Tea, however I have shut my Windows these 2 Nights and ye pain is almost gone Off, it never hurt my eating and Drinking.

Smith resigned from Congress in 1777 to return to his business affairs, which had suffered. His iron works were producing cannon shot for the Continental army but losing money, and many of his legal fees had remained uncollected. He followed the news of affairs around Philadelphia and was among the townspeople who greeted Congress' arrival in York Town that September. On December 10th, James Smith was re-elected to Congress, and he joined his compatriots on the 16th. He opened his law office as a meeting place for the Board of War. Upon the motion to return to Philadelphia in 1778, Smith returned with them, serving until October of that year.

Following his Congressional service, James Smith was elected to the Pennsylvania General Assembly, and in 1780, he was appointed a judge on the Pennsylvania High Court of Errors and Appeals. The following year, he was commissioned as a Brigadier General in the Pennsylvania militia. James Smith also played an important role in the settling of the boundary disputes between Pennsylvania and Connecticut.

During his later years, Smith's sense of patriotism focussed more locally, toward the development of his hometown. When York Town became a borough in 1787, Smith was one of the first councilmen. He served as the president of the York County Library Company and became a trustee of the York Academy in 1787 and its president in 1799, by which time it had become the York County Academy. He was also an early proponent of Pennsylvania's anti-slavery organizations. He retired from public life and his law practice in 1801.

James Smith's gravestone, placed by his son within the grounds of York's First Presbyterian Church, shows that he died at an advanced age. But, what age was he? His son reckoned that he was ninety-three, though he was more likely eighty-seven. Because he adamantly refused throughout his entire full and useful life to ever tell his real age, James Smith, York Town's own Jovial Eccentric, got in the last laugh.

Native Son of the Seat of Liberty

JONATHAN BAYARD SMITH

BIRTH: Philadelphia, Pennsylvania
February 21, 1742

DEATH: Philadelphia, Pennsylvania
June 16, 1812

COLONY: Pennsylvania

EDUCATION: College of New Jersey
(Princeton)

PROFESSION: Merchant, Politician

AT YORK TOWN: December 18, 1777,
until Adjournment

Jonathan Bayard Smith loved his native city of Philadelphia as much as he loved the idea of liberty and independence. If York Town may be styled the First Capital of the United States, certainly Philadelphia can be termed the Cradle of Liberty, and Smith would come to serve his country and his state in both cities.

Born into a mercantile family that had been transplanted from Portsmouth, New Hampshire, Smith was exposed quite early to sums, ledgers, ship's manifests, and a host of objects from countries far and wide. He, himself, was shipped abroad to England, no doubt to learn the trade from the perspective of the Atlantic Ocean's other side. Upon his return and subsequent graduation from the College of New Jersey in 1760, Smith was drawn more deeply into his family's business. But he was also drawn into other ventures, for he rallied to the cause of independence quite early and was counted among Philadelphia's most ardent patriots.

Smith's attention to details fostered by his upbringing, his quick mind and facile ability with a quill, and his zeal for the cause of Liberty were rewarded in 1775, when he was appointed secretary of Philadelphia's Committee of Safety. He served on that committee from 1775 to 1777. He was literally bursting with pride when the Declaration of Independence was first read in his city of Philadelphia the following year.

The next year, 1777, would be a most busy one for Smith. He was appointed Prothonotory of the Court of Common Pleas and was delighted when elected to the Continental Congress, too. But there were dark times ahead for Smith and his city. The British were rumored to be on their way to occupy Philadelphia and to drive Washington's army into defeat. On December 1, 1777, Smith chaired a meeting of Philadelphia's Whig faction, which had gathered to determine how best to handle the threat of English forces. Smith's position was as fervid as his patriotism, for he resolved "[t]hat it be recommended to the Council of Safety that in the great emergency . . . every person between the age of sixteen and fifty years be ordered out under arms." No "Sunshine Patriot" himself, he served a commission as a Lieutenant Colonel of a locally raised militia battalion commanded by his brother-in-law, Colonel John Bayard.

As Washington's demoralized troops huddled in misery at Valley Forge, Smith gave up his position in the field and took up his seat in Congress after a chilling trip to York Town. For this Philadelphian, his arrival at York Town's courthouse and the acceptance of his credentials must have been a bittersweet moment, knowing that his beloved city was suffering under British occupation. Yet no delegate could have been happier when, on June 27, 1778, Congress was ordered to reconvene in Philadelphia.

That year was also a busy one for Smith. He was reappointed to his Court of Common Pleas position and also named a Justice of Philadelphia's Court of Quarter Sessions and its Orphans' Court. Even more work was entrusted to him during later years. In 1781, he became an auditor for Pennsylvania's militia accounts. In 1794, Smith was elected Pennsylvania's Auditor General after, two years earlier, having been elected an alderman of his native city.

Smith served in capacities of honor beyond military and political involvements as well, and these demonstrate both the range of his interests and the depths of his abilities. He was a long-standing trustee of his alma mater, Princeton, and in 1779, he helped to found the University of the State of Pennsylvania, which in 1791 was merged into what became the University of Pennsylvania. In addition, Smith was a Grand Master Mason, Vice President of Philadelphia's Sons of Washington, and for forty years belonged to the American Philosophical Society.

Ardent patriot, successful politician and administrator, and multifaceted citizen, it was altogether fitting that Jonathan Bayard Smith, who was Philadelphia born and bred, should be laid to rest in Philadelphia soil on the grounds of the Second Presbyterian Church. He was truly a native son of the Seat of Liberty.

RHODE ISLAND

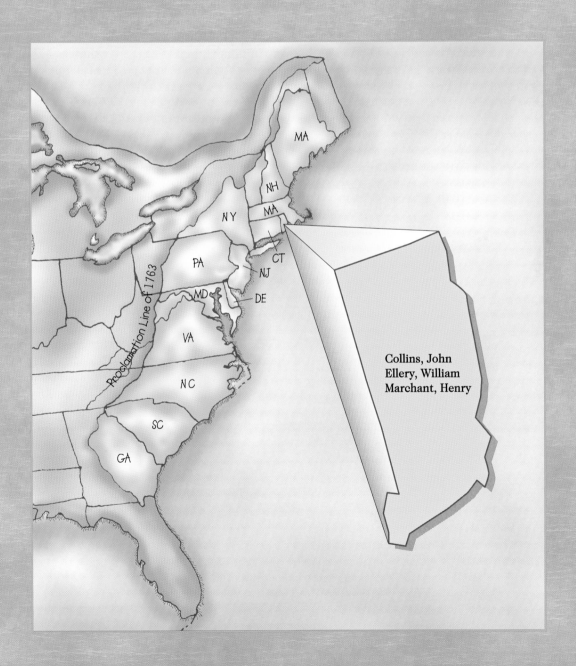

MA

NH

MA

N Y

PA

CT

NJ

MD

DE

Proclamation Line of 1763

VA

N C

SC

GA

Collins, John
Ellery, William
Marchant, Henry

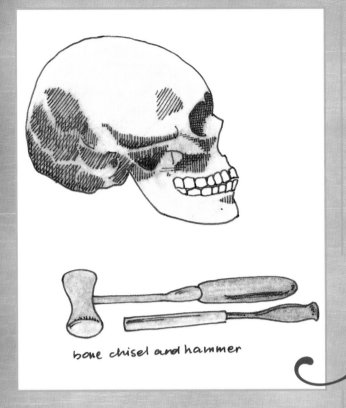

bone chisel and hammer

Admirer of George Washington

JOHN COLLINS

BIRTH: Newport, Rhode Island
November 1, 1717

DEATH: Newport, Rhode Island
March 4, 1795

COLONY: Rhode Island

EDUCATION: Local Schools

PROFESSION: Politician, Farmer

AT YORK TOWN: June 20, 1778, until
Adjournment

John Collins was an ardent patriot who, while quite willing to break loyalty with England, the Mother Country, found himself in a critical position where, despite great personal and political costs, he could not break loyalty with the man history would label as "the Father of our Country."

Collins was born in Newport decades before any thought was given to the idea of the tiny colony of Rhode Island becoming an independent state. While never far from the scent of salt air, Collins' own interests leaned toward farming the rich, glacially deposited soil that blanketed his homeland. Rhode Island farmers seemed to be a particularly fiercely independent lot, and as issues like the Stamp Act arose, Collins and many of his neighbors began to think about what was once considered to be unthinkable—independence. Mother England had become a far more domineering figure than a nurturing one, and that was hardly proper for a people growing toward a more advanced state of political maturity.

In 1776, as the clouds of war looked certain to break across the nearby Narragansett Sound, John Collins was honored to be appointed to a committee that set forth to meet with General George Washington. Their task was to ask his advice about how best to defend their coastline and to assemble their resources for the coming conflict. Collins' esteem for Washington grew even more on meeting this figure he had so admired from afar. Perhaps it was then that John Collins began to share more fully the vision that, once the British were defeated, the thirteen colonies were not destined to exist as thirteen independent states but, rather, to join permanently as a new nation. But not all his farming neighbors were willing to see that far.

John Collins was esteemed enough by his neighbors and kinsmen to be elected to represent them in Congress. So, after a long and dusty journey, he took his seat near the little courthouse's northern end on June 20th. He arrived in York Town months after the notorious Conway Cabal—the plot to replace Washington as Commander-in-Chief—but had he been there during those frigid February days when the conspirators were at their thickest, he certainly would have been a most vocal defender of Washington's cause. He served in Congress until 1777, when he was briefly replaced by William Ellery. He did not then know it, but the time was yet to come when he would be the most central figure in another controversy concerning anti-Washington opinions.

Collins was reelected to Congress in 1782 and 1783. Because he staunchly defended the agrarian constituency in their positions regarding the issuing of paper money and other matters, he was chosen to be Coroner of Rhode Island in 1786.

It is sometimes forgotten that not all the former colonies were thoroughly enamored with the idea of joining as a nation, and little Rhode Island fought vigorously against calling a national convention to adopt a Federal Constitution. It was at this time that Collins' admiration for Washington was severely tested. On the seventeenth day of a bleak January in 1790, Collins, as governor, found himself forced to act in the key role of President of the State Senate. That body was deadlocked on the issue of whether to participate in the Constitutional Convention. As he looked about the room of faces, he must have also seen, in his mind's eye, the faces of the many gritty Rhode Island farmers who were his neighbors—and who valued independence in all matters most of all. Here was the defining moment! John Collins cast his tie-breaking vote on the side of Federalism. He could, while others could not, see the value and the tremendous potential that George Washington had seen—that of a new nation, with liberty for all.

That vote, which cost him the esteem of many supporters and lost him the office of governor, was the climax of his political life. He was given the satisfaction of being elected as a representative of the new U.S. Congress, but he did not take his seat. Five years later, John Collins died and was laid to rest, a Washington admirer to his end, in the family cemetery at "Brenton Neck," his own beloved farm.

A Retiring Rhode Islander

WILLIAM ELLERY

BIRTH: Newport, Rhode Island
December 22, 1727

DEATH: Newport, Rhode Island
February 15, 1820

COLONY: Rhode Island

EDUCATION: Harvard

PROFESSION: Lawyer

AT YORK TOWN: November 7, 1777—
June 27, 1778

Great were the comings and goings to and from York Town in the autumn of 1777. As John Hancock, President of Congress, was leaving, William Ellery, delegate from Rhode Island, was coming. Their paths crossed at the Fishkill Ferry, New York. Ellery recorded the encounter in his diary:

> On our way to Fishkill Ferry we met President Hancock in a sulky, escorted by one of his secretaries and two or three other gentlemen, and one light horse-man (returning from Congress at York Town). The escort surprised us, as it seemed inadequate to the purpose, either of defense or parade. But our surprise was not of long circumstance; for we had not rode far before we met six or eight light horse-men on the canter, and just as we reached the Ferry, a boat arrived with many more—all making up the Escort of President Hancock. Who would not be a great man? I verily believe that the President, as he passed through the country thus escorted, feels a more triumphant satisfaction than the Colonel of the Queen's Regiment of Light Dragons attended by his whole army and escort of a thousand militia.

Because Ellery, traveling with his son-in-law, Francis Dana, and accompanied by a single man servant riding behind them, was making the 450-mile journey on horseback, the comparison is almost ludicrous. However, such pomp and panoply would have been entirely out of character for this plain-spoken, unassuming Newport lawyer. Although he had chosen law as his profession, his real love was the study of the Classics, especially the Greek and Latin languages. He displayed such strength and quiet courage in the Rhode Island resistance to British misrule, however, that he became a target for the English when they occupied Newport in 1776. His home was burned to the ground and other property destroyed.

Throughout his long career in Congress, he was more a silent observer than an activist, preferring to be in the background rather than the limelight. Even at the formal signing of the Declaration of Independence, he was more intent on observing his colleagues than anything else. During his later years, he was fond of narrating events of that great day as he remembered them:

> I was determined to see how they all looked, as they signed what might be their "death-warrant." I placed myself beside the Secretary, Charles Thomson, and eyed each closely as he affixed his name to the Document. Undaunted resolution was displayed on every countenance.

He relayed such news as the mistreatment of American prisoners by the British in Philadelphia and Washington's bleak prospects for the winter: "Our army will hut this winter at Valley Forge about twenty miles from Philadelphia and near Schuylkill." He also described his concern for the safety of Providence, Rhode Island, following the terms of the Saratoga Convention, "[b]y delaying the embarkation of Burgoyne's troops." He was afraid Providence might become the target of British resentment and the object of attack, and he convinced Congress about the necessity of keeping emergency troops on hand.

After the war, Ellery continued to be active in public service. In 1781, he was a Judge on the Supreme Court of Rhode Island and later worked with Rufus King of New York for the abolition of slavery. President Washington also appointed him Customs Collector for the port of Newport, a post he held for three decades.

William Ellery lived a long, fulfilling, and relatively happy life. He died at the age of ninety-two, sitting in his favorite chair while reading one of his favorite books—a work of Cicero—in the original Latin. He is to be remembered not so much for his own achievements as for his qualities of mind and spirit that made possible the achievements of others.

HENRY MARCHANT

BIRTH: Martha's Vineyard, Massachusetts
April 9, 1741

DEATH: Newport, Rhode Island
August 20, 1796

COLONY: Rhode Island

EDUCATION: Philadelphia College
(University of Pennsylvania)
LL.D., Yale University

PROFESSION: Lawyer, Jurist, Politician

AT YORK TOWN: October 1, 1777–
November 18, 1777
June 8, 1778, until
Adjournment

Some citizens rise to prominence by being a "big fish in a small pond," but it could be said of Henry Marchant that his prominence was sufficient to gain attention anywhere.

Marchant was the son of a sea captain, Hexford Marchant, whose vessel sailed from Martha's Vineyard. Young Henry bore the travail, not uncommon in those years, of losing his mother when he was but four years of age. His father moved his family to Newport after that and next married a daughter of Samuel Ward, whose family was most prominent in that colony. This connection proved beneficial to Henry through his later years.

Henry Marchant was schooled locally, then left the coastline of his adopted homeland for the seaport of Philadelphia, where he took up studies at Philadelphia College, which later became the University of Pennsylvania. After three years there, he returned to New England to read law under the great Edmund Trowbridge, one of the finest law preceptors in the country and the man who also taught Francis Dana, one of Marchant's close friends. But teacher and pupils did not see eye to eye when it came to politics, for Trowbridge was very conservative and Marchant and Dana both began developing ideas and interests that would mark them as patriots to the cause of independence.

Marchant kept in contact with his old college, and just as his legal and political career was beginning to blossom, he was also awarded an A.M. degree from Philadelphia College in 1762.

But Marchant's interests were not wholly focussed on the politics of the day, for he also enjoyed the company of a very intellectual, highly erudite pastor, Dr. Ezra Stiles. Indeed, in 1769, he assisted Stiles in observing and plotting the transit of the planet Venus, which demonstrates Marchant's keen abilities in science and higher mathematics.

Marchant's own political "star" continued to ascend when he was chosen as Rhode Island's Attorney General, and he served in that capacity from 1771 to 1776. He also embarked on other adventures, including travels to Britain, where he conducted business before the Privy Council, traveled through Scotland with Benjamin Franklin, and in the words of his loyal mentor, Dr. Stiles, "was personally acquainted with the Men of the first Eminence of Literature in Scotland and England."

He also moved more discreetly through another circle while overseas, for Marchant also came "in close touch with the merchants, non-conformists, and radicals who made up the 'friends of America' in Great Britain."

Shortly after his return to Rhode Island in 1772, he began to play a leading role in that colony's movement to gain independence. In May of 1773, Marchant was named to Rhode Island's Committee of Correspondence. The next year saw him on the committee to instruct delegates to the First Continental Congress, and he became a member of that body in 1776, having the previous year moved from Newport to his farm in South Kingston. While in Congress, Marchant served as a member of the Marine, Appeals, Treasury, and Southern Department Committees. He was pleased to be a signer of the Articles of Confederation, but shortly after his time in York Town, he began to focus more on issues and interests at home. Although re-elected to Congress in 1780 and 1783, he attended neither session, and when the 1784 term approached, Marchant resigned his seat, yielding the honor to another.

Between 1784 and 1790, he served as a member of Newport's General Assembly, and he was a leading voice in the local Federalist Party. He also served as a very vocal delegate to the Rhode Island State Convention to adopt the Federal Constitution in 1789.

Further honors awaited this great political figure, for he was appointed by President George Washington as judge of the U.S. District Court, serving between 1790 and 1796. He was also honored and proud to see his own son, William, graduate from Yale in 1792, and he shared one more "stellar" moment with his old mentor and friend, Dr. Ezra Stiles, when as President of Yale, Stiles placed the hood denoting the degree of LL.D. on Marchant's still-broad shoulders.

Henry Marchant went to his final rest on August 20, 1796, cradled in the rocky soil of the little state that he served so well for so long.

SOUTH CAROLINA

Drayton, William Henry
Heyward, Thomas, Jr.
Hutson, Richard
Laurens, Henry
Mathewes, John
Middleton, Arthur

WILLIAM HENRY DRAYTON

BIRTH: Drayton Hall, South Carolina
September 1742

DEATH: Philadelphia, Pennsylvania
September 3, 1779

COLONY: South Carolina

EDUCATION: Westminster School and
Balliol College, Oxford,
England

PROFESSION: Planter, Politician, Judge

AT YORK TOWN: March 30, 1778–
June 27, 1778

On March 22, 1778, Henry Laurens wrote to his son, John, at Valley Forge:

> Chief Justice Drayton and another, I believe Mr. Late Speaker Matthews, are on the road with mantles of Delegates to Congress. We certainly want members. The addition of abilities can never come amiss.

It was not long, however, before the varied and contradictory abilities of William Henry Drayton were going sorely "amiss" with Laurens himself. Drayton, a remarkable and controversial Carolinian, was an enigma to both friend and foe—and also probably to himself. Born to wealth, married to wealth (Dorothy Golightly, his wife), and made even wealthier through his own enterprise, he enjoyed all the power and privilege of his class. Like most British colonists, he was intensely loyal to the Crown and highly protective of his rights as a free-born Englishman.

At the first rumblings of dissent, most especially the boycott of merchants refusing to sign the non-importation agreement, Drayton stood firmly with the opposition. Unable to sell his own crops and disgusted that working men should dare to argue politics—even impose their will on "gentlemen"—he used his pen as a weapon of defense. Fighting a losing battle with South Carolina patriots, he went to England in 1770, where he published his diatribes against the "illegal" actions of his countrymen in a small book entitled *Letters of Freemen*.

This publication won him great favor at the Court of George III, where he was regarded as a possible future champion of British colonial authority. But they were wrong.

By 1776, Drayton was Chief Justice of South Carolina and a vigorous advocate of American independence. Still, the motives for his conversion were suspect. Were they self-serving or purely patriotic? Regardless of his motive, his zeal as a propagandist and his value to the cause of liberty were beyond question.

Drayton made his appearance in York Town when Congress was at its lowest ebb, both in numbers and in morale. Delegates were leaving at an alarming rate, and those remaining lacked the qualities of statesmanship characteristic of the original leaders. Petty bickering was dividing the House against itself. Small wonder that the weary, overworked President should find his brash and often high-handed "Converted Countryman" both difficult and annoying. Although they took opposite sides on many issues, the two Carolinians spoke with one voice against the British overtures for peace.

Only three weeks after Drayton's admission to Congress, Lord North's peace proposal arrived. Following General Washington's advice, Congress unanimously rejected it. William Drayton was one of a committee of three who drafted that rejection:

The committee beg leave to report it is their opinion that these United States cannot with propriety hold any conference or treaty with any commissioners on the part of Great Britain, unless they shall, as a preliminary thereto, either withdraw their fleets and armies, or else, in positive and express terms, acknowledge the independence of the said states.

With the adjournment of Congress to Philadelphia, the hostility with Laurens deepened, especially after the men took opposing sides in the Lee–Deane controversy. However, when Laurens learned that his fellow delegate had been stricken with typhus, he asked permission to visit. Their final meeting, according to Laurens, was entirely free of rancor:

When I approached the bed, he clasped my hand, and he wept affectingly; after recovering his voice, he signified great satisfaction at seeing me, and particularly requested that I write a state of his case to Mrs. Drayton.

William Henry Drayton died in Philadelphia on September 3, 1779 at the age of thirty-seven. He was buried the same day. Congress attended his funeral as a body, paying their last respects to their "Converted Countryman," whose patriotism was unquestionably sincere despite the fact that he loved controversy—and that it followed him throughout every stage of his career.

A Planter of Independence

THOMAS HEYWARD, JR.

BIRTH: Old House Plantation, St. Helena Parish, South Carolina
July 28, 1746

DEATH: St. Luke's Parish, South Carolina
March 6, 1809 or April 22, 1809

COLONY: South Carolina

EDUCATION: South Carolina, Middle Temple, London, England

OCCUPATION: Planter, Lawyer

AT YORK TOWN: September 30, 1777–
October 31, 1777
June 6, 1778–
June 28, 1778

The wealthy plantation owners of South Carolina planted more than rice on their vast acreage. They also sowed the seeds of a revolution that yielded the rich harvest of American independence. One of these was Thomas Heyward, Jr., the last survivor of the four South Carolina Signers.

Heyward's life followed much the same pattern as that of any other scion of a wealthy Southern family. He had the best classical education available locally, followed by enrollment in a British school or university, and topped off with a continental Grand Tour.

It was during his five years of study in England that the seeds of rebellion germinated in the mind of young Heyward. He could not bear the English policy of treating British colonial subjects as inferior to those born on English soil—a policy only too evident in the appointment of native Englishmen to governmental positions in the colonies. The exposure to the dazzling courts of Europe only deepened his resentment of tyranny and oppression.

When he returned home, he used every skill at his command to cultivate the seeds of resistance to British authority, which were already taking root in South Carolina soil. He was admitted to the Charleston Bar in 1771, and two years later, he married Elizabeth Mathewes, the sister of John Mathewes, who shared his political persuasion, and established his own household at White Hall Plantation. As a successful lawyer and wealthy planter, a man of influence and position, Heyward was a valuable asset to the First and Second Provincial Congress, to the Committee of Safety, and on the resignation of Christopher Gadsen, to the Second Continental Congress, where he signed his life-long commitment to independence. When Howe's occupation of Philadelphia forced the withdrawal of Congress to York Town, Heyward served there for a month as a member of the Committee for Foreign Affairs. It was his duty to inform the Commissioners at Paris on the progress of the War. During that fateful October, there was much to report—both good and bad. The good news was the progress of the northern army against Burgoyne. The bad news was the fall of Philadelphia and Washington's failures at Brandywine and Germantown. But the report of October 18th carried what was the most glorious and far-reaching news of all—the total surrender of Burgoyne at Saratoga.

Having been granted a leave of absence, Thomas Heyward left York Town on October 31st, the same day that John Hancock began his retirement as President of Congress. Without Heyward, South Carolina had no representatives in Congress except Henry Laurens, who was elected to replace Hancock as President. This situation, placing an extra burden on a sadly over-worked Laurens, remained unchanged until the arrival of Richard Drayton in the spring. Heyward did not return until June, and he took his final leave of Congress in August of 1778.

Back in South Carolina, this great liberalist took on the responsibilities of Judge of Criminal and Civil Courts and also joined the militia. In 1779, he was Captain of the Charleston Artillery Company. He was wounded in the Battle of Beaufort in 1779. As a Signer of the Declaration of Independence, a judge, and a well-known patriot, Heyward was a marked man when the British took Charleston the following year. As such, he suffered the fate of other prominent captives—imprisonment, exile in St. Augustine, and heavy property damage.

But worse was yet to come. He was exchanged as a prisoner of war in Philadelphia in 1782. Tragedy awaited him, for on her way to meet her husband, Elizabeth Heyward was taken ill and died.

After he retired from public life, Heyward settled down with his second wife, Elizabeth Savage, to enjoy the good life of a free man in a free society, the seeds of which he had helped to plant and nurture.

Today, his handsome townhouse at 87 Church Street in Charleston is open to the public. Because it was President Washington's headquarters during his visit in 1791, it is known as the Heyward–Washington House and is a popular tourist attraction. Visitors are impressed by the three-story Georgian mansion, especially the elaborate second-floor drawing room, furnished with period pieces and the family china.

The name of Thomas Heyward is recognized and revered far beyond the borders of South Carolina. Not only, as the monument on his grave at Old House Plantation attests, is he honored as "patriot, statesman, soldier, Jurist," but most truly as "Husbandman of American Liberty."

Cut From a Different Cloth

RICHARD HUTSON

BIRTH: Prince William Parish, South
      Carolina
      July 9, 1748

DEATH: Charleston, South Carolina
      April 12, 1795

COLONY: South Carolina

EDUCATION: Princeton

OCCUPATION: Lawyer

AT YORK TOWN: May 13, 1778–
             June 28, 1778

Unlike the other South Carolina patriots, Richard Hutson was not born to wealth or social position. He was not the son of a rich plantation owner, nor did he marry into one of the First Families of the South. In fact, he did not marry at all.

From all accounts, his father, William Hutson, came to South Carolina from England in 1740, and although trained as a lawyer, he joined a troop of strolling players performing at the Dock Street Theater in Charleston. His career as an actor came to an abrupt end, however, when he fell under the spell of the English evangelist George Whitfield. Not only was he converted to the Calvinistic Methodist faith, he became a teacher at Bethesda Orphanage, founded by Whitfield in Savannah in 1740. When the Independent Church of Indian Lands was organized in 1743, William Hutson was its first pastor.

When Richard Hutson was born, he inherited three things from his father—a deep respect and passion for learning, an innate interest in law, and a commitment to the dis-establishment of the Anglican Church. After his graduation from Princeton in 1765, he became a successful and prosperous lawyer in Charleston. In politics, he became a stalwart opponent of the Stamp Act. His outspoken opposition to all acts of British aggression won him the reputation of an uncompromising revolutionist.

Hutson served in the militia, was elected to several assemblies, and was a delegate to Congress in 1774, 1776, and 1778. When he returned to South

Carolina in 1778, he suffered the same fate as his fellow patriots—capture and imprisonment by the British under Sir Henry Clinton. But, even while a prisoner of war in St. Augustine, Hutson showed his strong individualism by using his time to a distinct advantage. He turned his mind to the study of the Spanish language and, by the time of his release, had become quite proficient in this foreign tongue.

Hutson, like most other patriots, paid a high price for victory. The considerable fortune he had been able to amass was seriously depleted, and he found himself facing financial ruin. His dilemma was made even worse by his insisting on taking payment for moneys owed him in continental currency, hoping by his example to strengthen government credit. However, his personal problems did not interrupt his service to state and country. He became Chancellor of South Carolina in 1784, Senior Judge of the Chancery Court in 1791, and a member of the State Convention for ratifying the Federal Constitution in 1788.

Although Richard Hutson appeared to be cut from a different cloth, the fabric of his soul contained the same strong threads that bound all of the South Carolina patriots together as brothers in the cause of American independence.

The Man Nearest the Fire

ENRY LAURENS

BIRTH: Charleston, South Carolina
      March 6, 1724

DEATH: Charleston, South Carolina
      December 8, 1792

COLONY: South Carolina

EDUCATION: Business

PROFESSION: Merchant

AT YORK TOWN: September 30, 1777–
      June 28, 1778

When Henry Laurens accepted the gavel from retiring President John Hancock, he commented that at least his seat would be nearer to the fire. Taken literally, this meant he would be closer to the small iron stove in the center of the room. Even though it was only the first of November, the delegates in York County's drafty court house pulled the green baize table covers closer around their shanks and used their foot-warmers to ward off the chill. Taken figuratively, the remark was symbolic of the raging conflict sweeping the nation, and Henry Laurens would soon find himself in the center of that conflagration.

First, there were the long and heated debates over the Articles of Confederation. Next were the smoking guns of Saratoga. Then came the boiling cauldron of intrigue—plot and counter-plot of pro- and anti-Washington factions—and, finally, the hot and heavy controversy between Arthur Lee and Silas Deane, which ultimately led to the resignation of Laurens two years later.

There is no question that Henry Laurens was more than equal to his task, although it turned out to be a greater burden than even he anticipated. As he listened to the seemingly endless arguments over the Articles, he became increasingly aware of the strong party divisions among the Congress. As he wrote to his good friend John Lewis Gervais, who managed his business affairs during his absence:

Congress is not the respectable body which I expected to have found. When I first arrived here, I was told, by way of caution, that there were <u>parties</u>. I found <u>parties</u> within <u>parties</u>, divisions and subdivisions to as great a possible extent as the number thirty-five (we never have more than that together) will admit of.

As it is wholly contrary to my genius or practice to hold with any of them as party, so I incur the censure of not belonging with any.

But there was no division on the only item of business transacted during the new President's first day in office—the resolution to set aside Thursday, December the 18th, as a day of national thanksgiving for the glorious victory at Saratoga, which was unanimously passed. Even so, by the time that first national Thanksgiving Day rolled around, Congress was facing the dilemma of the Saratoga Convention, and Henry Laurens was again in the "hot seat." Because of his high standards of personal honor, he truly agonized over a decision that would render the crafty Burgoyne powerless to re-assemble his troops to "fight another day," but that still might be interpreted by the rest of the world as a breach of public faith.

His misery was compounded by a bad attack of gout. He had to hobble on crutches or be carried over the ice and snow from Eva Swope's boarding house on Market Street to the Courthouse where he sat, wrapped in blankets, deliberating over the precarious affairs of state.

And precarious they were, and made even more so by the growing dissatisfaction with Washington as Commander-in-Chief. It was the victory at Saratoga, making Horatio Gates the Man of the Hour, who proved to be the tinderbox, kindling the fires of envy and ambition that threatened to consume Washington and all around him.

Laurens was in a key position to find out exactly what was going on. His beloved son, John, a close friend of Lafayette and a protege of Washington, was at camp in Valley Forge. Both young men were ardent supporters of their Commander-in-Chief.

It was this triumvirate—Henry Laurens, Colonel John Laurens, and the Marquis de Lafayette—who helped extinguish the bonfire of conspiracy before it could destroy the man they so loved and admired. The scheme to replace General Washington with General Gates, hatched by Washington's enemies in Congress and the Board of War, is known as *the Conway Cabal.* It was named for Thomas Conway, an unscrupulous, ambitious Irish volunteer who had been elevated to the rank of Brigadier General over the expressed objections of Washington. To what extent General Gates was actually involved was never fully determined, either by Laurens or by those who came after him. Suffice to say, the Conway Cabal is now only a footnote to history.

When Congress left York in 1778, Laurens had every reason to be proud. The Articles of Confederation had been completed, the army reorganized and revitalized, the British peace proposals rejected, and the French Treaties of Alliance and Commerce signed and sealed. In the absence of an official United States seal, those documents bear the personal seal of Henry Laurens.

Laurens continued to serve as President of Congress until his resignation in 1779, but he remained in the service of his country. In fact, it could be said that his resignation plunged him "from the frying pan into the fire." In 1780, he was appointed Minister to Holland. En route, his vessel, the *Mercury,* was captured by the British, and Laurens was held prisoner in the Tower of London for more than a year. Although he was finally exchanged for Lord Cornwallis, the worst was yet to come. On August 12, 1782, he received a mandate from Congress to join the Peace Commissioners in Paris. But by the same post, he received the deathblow to all of his personal hopes and dreams. A letter from John Adams informed him that his son John, whom he had last seen on the day of his embarkation, had been killed in a skirmish at Combahee Ferry, August 27th. The death of Colonel John Laurens was said to be the last casualty of the war.

Laurens lived for ten more years at "Mepkin," his plantation, but his health had been undermined by his imprisonment. His will contained the request that his body be wrapped in twelve yards of tow cloth and burned until it should be entirely and totally consumed, and that his bones be deposited wherever considered proper. His last wishes were faithfully carried out—the first recorded cremation on American soil—and his ashes buried beside the grave of his son. The fire that consumed the body of Henry Laurens was no cleaner or brighter than the fire of patriotism that, for sixty-nine years, burned in the heart of this truly great American.

Devoted Public Servant

JOHN MATHEWES

BIRTH: Charleston, South Carolina
    1744

DEATH: Charleston, South Carolina
    October 26, 1802 or
    November 17, 1802

COLONY: South Carolina

EDUCATION: Local schools, Middle
    Temple, London

PROFESSION: Lawyer, Planter, Politician

AT YORK TOWN: April 22, 1778, until
    Adjournment

From Ensign in the militia during the Cherokee War of 1760 to Governor of his state in 1782, and in other important capacities until his death, John Mathewes (also spelled Matthewes, Matthews) dedicated himself to the affairs of South Carolina. A precocious patriot, he was campaigning against Indians at sixteen, admitted to practice law at the prestigious Middle Temple at twenty, and became a member of South Carolina's Bar at twenty-one. It is as if he could barely wait to enter public service.

Mathewes lost no time in joining the revolutionary movement. Aided by the record of service he demonstrated when earlier elected to the Royal Assembly of South Carolina, he represented his home territory of St. John Colleton Parish in the First Provincial Congress of 1775. He was re-elected to the Second Provincial Congress the following year but resigned to take up a judgeship. He was next elected to the Second General Assembly, serving as Speaker between December 6, 1776, and September 12, 1777. His subsequent election as a delegate brought him to York Town, far from the balmy clime of his homeland.

As an ardent Whig, Mathewes was noted in Congress as displaying "much energy, eloquence, and general legislative ability," adding greatly to his reputation, which was of a quality to ensure his continued election as a delegate and his subsequent election as Governor of South Carolina in 1782. During his one-year term as Governor, he was re-elected to the Privy Council, and he enjoyed, with great patriotic pleasure, watching the British evacuate his state once and for all.

However, this devoted public servant's work was far from done. John Mathewes continued to be re-elected as a member of the General Assembly and was chosen as a member of the convention to ratify the U.S. Constitution. Considered "a man of high talent, firm and resolute will, and of extensive information," he was often tapped to lend his expertise in local matters, ranging from service as a Justice of the Peace to his appointment as a road commissioner, a militia captain, a trustee for the College of Charleston, and a committeeman to study the Jay Treaty of 1795. He also served as a judge until his death in 1802.

John Mathewes, ever busy, found the time for civil and social involvements as well. He was a long-standing member of the St. Andrews Society and the Charleston Library Society, and in 1786, he was a founder of Charleston's St. George's Club and served as president of the American Revolution Society.

It is well that Mathewes, so precocious and esteemed, launched himself into his role of public servant when he did, for it can be said that the able man died far too young. He was only fifty-eight at his death, and only three years earlier, he had taken a second wife, Sarah Rutledge, who followed Mary, his devoted first wife of more than thirty years. John Mathewes had served South Carolina for three-quarters of his life.

ARTHUR MIDDLETON

BIRTH: Middleton Place, Charleston, South Carolina
June 26, 1742

DEATH: Charleston, South Carolina
January 1, 1787

COLONY: South Carolina

EDUCATION: Cambridge, England

OCCUPATION: Planter, Politician

AT YORK TOWN: September 30, 1777–
October 16, 1777

Henry Middleton began laying out his vast, formal gardens at Middleton Place on the Ashley River in 1741, just a year before the birth of his son, Arthur. Today, the sixty-five acres of waterways, terraces, and flowering plants, arranged in elaborate geometric patterns, constitute the oldest landscaped garden in the United States. But Middleton Place is not only a garden masterpiece. A year-round Mecca for tourists, it is also a living monument to one of the wealthiest and most patriotic families in Colonial America.

Henry Middleton was, indeed, a MAN OF PROPERTY, with enormous holdings throughout the Carolinas, England, and the Barbados, and he had a strong sense about the responsibility such wealth entailed. He ensured that his son received an education befitting a gentleman of substance, culture, and scholarship by sending the boy to England at the age of twelve to begin his studies.

Young Arthur proved himself a serious and able student, and after completing his work at Cambridge and the Middle Temple, he rounded out his education with a Grand Tour of the continent. He returned home at the age of twenty-two as a handsome and highly eligible bachelor in Charleston society, and he soon lost his heart to the beautiful and wealthy Mary (Polly) Izard, whom he married in August of 1764. The young couple took up residence in the great Georgian mansion at Middleton Place. But even such a romantic existence amid idyllic surroundings did not preclude his participation in the real world. His influential friends and neighbors were quick to recognize his legal knowledge and social position as qualifications for public office, and they elected him as a member of the 27th Royal Assembly as well as Justice of the Peace for Berkley County.

In 1768, Arthur Middleton's active mind and love of learning inspired him to take his young family to Europe for an extended visit during which he devoted himself to the study of art and literature and developed into quite an accomplished painter. By the time they returned in 1771, however, South Carolina was a hotbed of political dissension toward England, but there was never any doubt where Arthur Middleton would stand in the melee. Despite close family ties with the Royal Governor, Lord William Campbell, Middleton participated in a raid to seize arms stores before the Governor could confiscate them. He was an ardent supporter of armed resistance and helped raise funds for that purpose. He also served in the First and Second Provincial Assemblies, the Committee of Safety, and wrote several political essays under the pseudonym of Andrew Marvell.

Middleton was a violent opponent of the Royalists, advocating that they be tarred and feathered, and he supported confiscating the estates of Tories who left the country. In the spring of 1776, he was chosen to replace his more conservative father in the Continental Congress—and arrived in time to immortalize the family name by affixing it to the Declaration of Independence.

The following year—the Year of the Hangman—Middleton left Philadelphia and, together with Thomas Heyward and Henry Laurens, represented South Carolina at the first session of the Continental Congress that reconvened at York Town. His stay, however, was too brief for him to have much influence in the weighty business transacted during those sessions.

His departure from Congress did not mean his removal from the war effort. He immediately returned to the South Carolina legislature, but his main concern was the British threat to Charleston. That threat became a reality in 1780, and after removing his family outside the city, he joined the militia in its defense. When the city fell, he was one of the four South Carolina Signers captured and exiled to St. Augustine, Florida, and was afterward confined on the prison ship *Jersey*. He was exchanged in 1781 and again served in Congress from 1781 to 1783. But, even after the end of the war, Arthur Middleton continued his fight for justice by fiercely contesting the exchange of Cornwallis as a prisoner of war. He even submitted such a resolution to Congress; "That Cornwallis should be regarded as a barbarian, who had violated all the rules of modern warfare, and had been guilty of innumerable cases of wanton cruelty and oppression." Although Arthur Middleton's losses were heavy during the war, including property vandalism by the British, he continued to maintain a magnificent lifestyle until his death at the age of forty-four. He left his wife with eight children—to quote one modern voice, "all boys except six!"

The gardens at Middleton Place have survived in all their splendor, but the house was not so fortunate. Not only did it fall victim to British vandalism, it was also completely burned during the War Between the States. Only a 20th-century renovation of the South Wing remains.

Present-day tourists exclaim in delight over the glories of Middleton Place—the flaming colors of its flowering plants, the majesty of its thousand-year-old live oak, the magnificence of its superb terraces and Butterfly Lakes. But a hush falls over those who pause at the family graveyard and mausoleum as they pay silent tribute to a father and son who gave, unstintingly, of themselves, their courage, their wealth, and their counsel to their country in its greatest time of need.

$\mathcal{V}$IRGINIA

Adams, Thomas
Banister, John
Harrison, Benjamin
Harvie, John
Jones, Joseph
Lee, Francis Lightfoot
Lee, Richard Henry

A Virginia Merchant

THOMAS ADAMS

BIRTH: New Kent County, Virginia
1730

DEATH: Augusta County, Virginia
October, 1788

COLONY: Virginia

EDUCATION: Local tutors

PROFESSION: Merchant

AT YORK TOWN: April 16, 1778, until
Adjournment

Thomas Adams often handled his family's business ventures from afar while his older brother, Richard, handled the Virginia end. They also followed this arrangement when it came to serving Virginia's bid for independence. Richard was often elected to local offices, while Thomas was the one who traveled afar to take a seat in Congress at York Town.

Thomas Adams, son of the transplanted English merchant Ebenezer Adams, was born in New Kent County, Virginia, in 1730, four years after his elder brother, Richard. Although they were Ebenezer's fourth and fifth sons, they became the two who operated their family's extensive mercantile trade on their maturity. Adams grew up around the business and was first drawn to put his acumen to work as clerk of Henrico County in 1753, an appointment given him when merely twenty-two or twenty-three years old. Four years later, he was elected to the vestry of Henrico Parish.

All the while, the family business grew substantially. It was determined that Thomas should facilitate things in the "Mother Country" and, thus, moved to London in about 1762. He took up residence on or near Fleet Street to keep his eyes and ears open to the doings of that great financial capitol. He often received mail posted to "The Virginia Coffee House" and other such gathering spots. Meanwhile, the expatriate "Virginia Merchant" held his county clerkship position by employing a deputy, while his brother, Richard, maintained the home affairs and entered into local politics.

Thomas Adams gathered a very interesting perspective on the growing clouds of revolution while in London, and he must have longed to be back in Virginia. He wrote in the summer of 1769 that he was "[h]eartily tired of doing Business in London." While there, he did take pleasure in recommending the requests of a family friend (and customer!) to a London firm, as being a gentleman of character and abilities. His name? Thomas Jefferson, Esq. As Adams wrote in 1770:

> There is no man living who I wish more to oblige as I think there is none of greater merit. He is a Counselor at Law and a shining ornament to it.

Almost one year later, Jefferson wrote to Thomas Adams, this time with a request for household and personal items to furnish his Monticello estate:

> I wrote therein for a Clavichord. I have since seen a Forte-piano and am charmed with it. Send me this instrument instead of the Clavichord: let the case be of fine mahogany, solid not veneered, the compass from Double G to F, in alt, a plenty of spare strings; and the workmanship of the whole very handsome and worthy the acceptance of a lady for whom I intend it.

Adams finally returned to Virginia in time to take an active role in forwarding the cause of Revolution. In 1774, he presided "in the chair" of New Kent County's meetings to select delegates to attend the first Virginia Convention. He, himself, would be elected to Virginia's House of Burgesses, and in 1777, he was named to the Governor's advisory board, the Council of State.

In December, 1777, Adams was elected to Congress. Upon his arrival at York Town, he was immediately named to the committees of Commerce, Marine Affairs, and Indian Affairs. He is described as one who "attended Congress faithfully." His position was an interesting one, because being fairly new to politics, he did not have a lot of political enemies, nor was he immediately associated with any of the numerous "factions" that kept debates lively. He did tend to side against the Lee Family, deeply involved in the controversy over Silas Dean's doings in France. Indeed, Richard Lee wrote to Adams on June 27, 1777, and the tone of his words was rather prickly:

> If America would exert itself, these invaders [the British] might be driven off the continent. Our country seems to be asleep and I think our government wants energy. If you have a spare moment, I shall be glad to hear from you.

When it came time for Virginia to re-elect its delegates, Thomas Adams, again because of his generally neutral positions, found himself becoming the chairman of the Virginia members of Congress. He served diligently until his vast family business could no longer do without him. He first took a four-month leave, but then he finally resigned from Congress on April 28, 1779.

Adams moved to a substantial estate in Augusta County, Virginia, and served there as a Justice of the County Court. He also served as a state senator from 1783 to 1786 and acted on a variety of local committees. The closing years of Thomas Adams' life are obscure. This "Virginia Merchant" and staunch patriot, who was described as "a man of great intelligence and benevolence," died at his home. His exact date of death is unknown, and his gravesite has been lost.

Congressman–Colonel–Mayor

JOHN BANISTER

BORN: Bristol Parish, Virginia
December 26, 1734

DIED: Buried–Dinwiddie County, Virginia
near Petersburg, Virginia
September 30, 1788

COLONY: Virginia

EDUCATION: England, read law at Temple
Bar, London

PROFESSION: Planter, Businessman

AT YORK TOWN: April 16, 1778–
June 27, 1778

Few delegates who arrived in York Town had a family lineage with roots embedded more deeply in England's history than those of John Banister, whose ancestors' loyalties to Richard III were recorded in 1484. Yet a sense of adventure and curiosity, which evidently became a family trait, lured Banister's grandfather, also named John, to the New World in the 17th century's last years.

This elder John Banister was a noted botanist and naturalist who also helped lay out, in 1732, a new village on the Appomattox River named Petersburg. This John Banister, who was noted as a Virginia colonist and Petersburg founder, died in an accident while collecting botanical samples at the falls of Roanoke long before his grandson, John, would become noted as one of the founders of a new nation.

The younger John Banister was dispatched to England to be educated, and after learning the profession of law at London's Temple Bar, he returned to Virginia, to his family's flourishing plantation and the growing village his grandfather had helped found. Because of his family's position and wealth and his own astute mind and popularity, he entered local politics, where he was first elected to the Virginia Convention of 1776. The following year, he became a member of Virginia's House of Burgesses.

John Banister, like his grandfather, enjoyed the ability to simultaneously pursue multiple interests. He developed a profitable milling complex near his home, and as millers were often wont to do, Banister chose to reflect his wealth by building a substantial mansion house. This was no ordinary mansion, but one designed in the latest of styles. Battersea House, started in 1768, was modeled after the fine Palladian country homes that dotted the English landscapes throughout the early and mid-18th century. Banister's home also had a distinctive feature that even further exhibited its owner's refined sense of fashion—a Chippendale-styled staircase that incorporated Chinese decorative motifs.

Banister, most decidedly, was open to things new, so it should be no surprise that he avidly embraced the patriot cause. Yet he also had strong military interests, too, and he visited the new American army's headquarters about the time of the battle of Germantown. He then formed an attachment to the idea of campaigning.

As a member of Congress, Banister fled to York Town and soon took to the duties at hand of shaping a government's legislation and of reshaping a demoralized army. He was one of the delegates who visited Washington's encampment as a member of the Committee of Arrangements. He was also a signer of the Articles of Confederation and an ardent supporter of the pursuit of liberty for all. While in Congress, he joined Patrick Henry in opposing the plan of Peyton Randolph to establish a banking system that Henry described as being "a scheme to reclaim the spendthrift from his dissipation and extravagance by filling his pockets with money." He also supported, as a plantation owner himself, the plan Thomas Jefferson forwarded to the Virginia Assembly to emancipate slaves—a proposal that failed.

But Banister would lay aside the mantle of Congressman and don a new one, that of a Lieutenant Colonel of cavalry under General Lawson,

between 1778 and 1781. This was within the time of him suffering the ignominy of having his own plantation occupied by Benedict Arnold's British forces, who had landed at City Point to invade Virginia. Although after Lawson's command was broken up and Banister was left without a detachment to lead, he still found ways to aid the army he came to love. His plantation was continuously ravaged by British forces, but he still found money to help equip General Greene's forces with blankets at his own expense, and he also converted his flour mills to make gunpowder for his intrepid colleagues in the field.

Few rejoiced with more fervor than John Banister when Cornwallis surrendered at Yorktown, and his new nation's future was secured. He returned to Battersea and enjoyed a rejuvenated prosperity. He also enjoyed his marriage to a second wife, Anna, the daughter of another esteemed Virginia family, and the thriving of his children by that union. In later life, he was called on to be a delegate of Dinwiddie Parish in the convention to reorganize the Episcopal Church, and in a gesture that surely would have pleased his grandfather, John Banister was named Petersburg's first mayor, demonstrating that his interests in the community the elder John helped to lay out had never waned.

John Banister was laid to rest, after a diverse, productive life, in 1788. He would have been saddened to learn that his beloved plantation would, yet again, be touched by armies in the field. During America's Civil War, the Confederate defenses surrounding Petersburg and Richmond passed near enough that both Blue and Grey soldiers marched through. But the elder John Banister, the naturalist, would have been delighted that his grandson, John, managed to have a small stream in Halifax County named for his distinguished elder—the Congressman, Colonel, and Mayor.

The Falstaff of Congress

BENJAMIN HARRISON

BIRTH: Berkeley Plantation, Charles City County, Virginia
April 5, 1726

DEATH: City Point, Prince George County, Virginia
April 24, 1791

COLONY: Virginia

EDUCATION: William and Mary (was not graduated)

PROFESSION: Plantation owner

AT YORK TOWN: September 30, 1777– October 9, 1777

From all descriptions, Benjamin Harrison did indeed bear a certain physical resemblance to Shakespeare's comic figure. He was overweight, jolly, jocular, and he loved to eat, drink, and be merry, but the baser nature of Shakespeare's character was totally missing. He was, most surely, neither a boaster nor a womanizer, nor did he take advantage of the poverty or gullibility of others who were less fortunate.

As the descendant of an established Virginia family and the son of a wealthy plantation owner, young Harrison was enrolled at William and Mary College, but he failed to take his degree. According to some sources, he left college to take over the management of his father's estate; other sources claim that he was either expelled or quit because of a violent disagreement with a professor. In either case, after his father and two sisters were killed by a bolt of lightning, he inherited the responsibility of the estate—as well as that of becoming a member of the House of Burgesses. In the controversy over the Stamp Act, the Royal Governor invited the influential young man to a seat in his council, a position that Harrison promptly refused, espousing instead the revolutionary party. He served as one of the committeemen who drew up a protest but later refused to endorse Patrick Henry's resolution for civil disobedience as a countermeasure.

He was elected to the First Continental Congress in 1774. There, in Philadelphia, the southern patriots came face to face with their New England counterparts. In their first dinner together at the City Tavern, they took each other's measure. Despite their surface differences, their common dedication to the cause of liberty ensured mutual acceptance. As Page Smith put it in his biography of John Adams, "The grand airs of the Virginians thus appeared as brotherly warmth, and the coldness of the Massachusetts men was taken for Republican simplicity."

Re-elected to the Second Continental Congress, Harrison abandoned his conservatism, seeing the necessity of complete independence from Great Britain, and became one of the signers of the Declaration of Independence in August of 1776. Contrary to the estimate of John Adams, that he was "an indolent, luxurious, heavy gentleman . . . of no use to Congress," Harrison proved to be a non-vocal but loyal and exceedingly useful member, especially to the Committee of Foreign Affairs.

He was also an extremely loyal supporter of George Washington. Although he retired from Congress in 1777 and resumed his seat in the House of Burgesses, he kept in touch with the doings of Congress and was well aware of the conspiracy to replace Washington with Gates. In an exchange of confidence with Robert Morris on February 19, 1778, he wrote, in part:

> It gives one great pain to be certainly inform'd that there are some in the Senate who dislike our General. I have long suspected it, nay, something more than suspect it, but had my hopes that his continued Labours, and the situation he has ever been in, of always being inferiour to the Enemy in numbers, and his men in want of

every necessary, circumstances well-known to Congress, would in the end have made every man his friend, and would have satisfied them that more than he has done would not have been done, by any man, and that we have no one that in any degree could have equal'd him; I am as confident of this as I am of my existence that the Favorite of the Day is as far inferiour to him as he is Inferiour to any officer in the Army, and this truth America will experience to her cost, if ever he should be placed at the head of her armies. Certain I am of one thing, that if this measure takes place, a great part of the strength of this country will be taken off.

He concluded these heartfelt opinions with the perceptive warning: "BEWARE YOUR BOARD OF WAR."

He was Speaker of the House of Burgesses until his election as Governor in 1782. After his second term as Governor, he retired to private life until 1791, when he was elected to serve a third term. On the evening after his election, he invited a party of friends to dine with him. During the course of the celebration, although he was just recovering from an attack of "[g]out of the stomach," he over-indulged in true Falstaffian tradition—and he died on the following day.

Benjamin Harrison loved all the good things in life, but most of all, he loved his country—and proved it by his unquestioned loyalty and devotion. At least he surpassed his friendly critic and co-patriot, John Adams, on one score. He was not only the father of a President of the United States, William Henry Harrison, but also the great-grandfather of another, his namesake and our 23rd President, Benjamin Harrison.

JOHN HARVIE

BIRTH: Albemarle County, Virginia
1742

DEATH: Richmond, Virginia
February 6, 1807

COLONY: Virginia

EDUCATION: No records

OCCUPATION: Lawyer, Businessman,
Builder

AT YORK TOWN: October 16, 1777–
January 23, 1778
February 27, 1778–
March 1778

John Harvie was born in 1742 and Thomas Jefferson in 1743. But the Harvie–Jefferson Connection began long before the birth of either one, for their fathers were good friends.

In 1757, the year of Peter Jefferson's death, Colonel John Harvie was named as the executor of Jefferson's will and also as one of the guardians of his fourteen-year-old son, Thomas. Three years later, it was to Colonel Harvie that young Tom sent his urgent request to further his education at William and Mary College. With the request granted, the seventeen-year-old Jefferson was duly enrolled in that institution.

No such specifics are available for the education of the eighteen-year-old John Harvie, but wherever and however acquired, it prepared him to practice law, to engage in business, and to construct public buildings as well as private residences in Richmond.

Like his father, John Harvie took a lively interest in public affairs during the era of the Revolution. He recruited troops, was a member of the Virginia Assembly, served in the Virginia Conventions of 1775 and 1776, and was active in the settlement of Indian affairs, most especially in the treaty negotiations at Fort Pitt.

By the time Harvie began his career at Congress in October of 1777, Jefferson had finished his own there and had become a member of the Virginia House of Delegates. The two Virginians remained in close contact. Harvie's letters from York Town were more than reports of official business. They contained such important news as Burgoyne's surrender at Saratoga, but they were, for the most part, outpourings of a more intimate and personal nature. For example, Harvie criticized Congress:

> I have not yet had a very clear, distinct view of Congress, but have seen and heard enough to Convince me that it is not that Wise, Systematic decent Assembly that you knew tow [sic] (two) years ago . . . Rely on it our Confederacy is not founded on Brotherly Love, and Able Statesmen are surely wanting here. The supporters of this government are a set of weak men without any Weight of Character.

Harvie also expressed his views on the dangerous prevalence of AVARICE:

> The avarice of Individuals will be more Fatal to the Liberties of America than the Sword of the Enemy! The avarice and disaffection of the people here is so great that they refuse any price that we can give for the necessary provisions for the Army, and the General's [Washington] last Letter, couched in terms Strong and pathetic, holds out a probability of the Army's dissolving unless they are more fully and Constantly supplied.

Harvie even questioned his personal suitability for Congress:

> To make room (for more qualified delegates) I will with pleasure resign if you advise me that it will not be imputed to unworthy motives. That would Restrain me, if the service were as bitter as Gall. But to you who know me so well, it is needless to say I do not possess talents for State Affairs, and yet truly I am one of the Board of War without having the skill in Military Affairs of an Orderly Sergeant!

He had regrets at being unable to find the skilled workmen Jefferson needed for construction at Monticello:

> This gives me uneasiness, as there is no man on Earth for whom I would Execute a Trust with greater Pleasure.

He wrote of his confidences regarding family concerns:

> My situation is disagreeable here . . . sometimes the Cares of a Husband and parent tell me there is a duty owing to them as well as to my Country. I beseech you not to consider this Sentiment as arising from a littleness of Soul, or a Sordid Spirit, but I could not be just to the Woman who devoted herself to me if I now altogether neglected the Interests of her and the little Pledges she has presented me with. The complications of this letter will convince you of the respect I must have for the man to whom I open my whole Soul without Ceremony, Punctilio or reserve.

There is no doubt that Harvie saw Jefferson, though a year his junior, in the role of elder statesman and personal mentor.

In spite of his distaste for the job, Harvie performed his duties to the letter. He spent almost a month at Valley Forge and was a first-hand observer of the hardships endured by Washington and his troops. He was also a member of almost every committee appointed to secure provisions for the army. He was named to the Committee of Appeals, the Maritime Committee, and also the Committee of Commerce.

Harvie cast his last vote in Congress on September 28th, 1778, and departed for Virginia soon afterward. As a private citizen, he returned to the two activities he most enjoyed—business and building. He served as purchasing agent for Virginia and as the Register of the Land Office for many years. He also resumed his career as a builder and, in his later years, served as Mayor of Richmond.

The lives of John Harvie and Thomas Jefferson continued to touch each other, and sometimes in unexpected ways. While in Congress, Harvie had opposed the delay of Burgoyne's return to England, a stipulation of the Saratoga Convention. But at the same time, he took an interest in the dispersal of Hessian prisoners, especially those moved from Massachusetts to Virginia. Accordingly, he donated a large tract of land four miles west of Monticello as a campsite. When Jefferson visited the camp in December of 1779, he was horrified by conditions there—incomplete barracks, exposure to the elements, and decayed food. He immediately enlisted aid for improvements. He also made friends with some of the officers, particularly Major General Frederick Adolph Riedesel who, with his wife and children, were frequent guests at Monticello.

John Harvie lived to see his friend and confidante become the third President of the United States. He died in 1807 at Belvedere, his home, due to a fall sustained while inspecting a Richmond mansion later known as the Gamble House.

It is accurate to say that Thomas Jefferson was the lodestar of his life. Harvie was devoted not only to the man himself, but to his ideals of independence and government as well. America and Jefferson, too, had no more faithful friend than John Harvie.

JOSEPH JONES

BIRTH: King George County, Virginia
      1727

DEATH: Fredericksburg, Virginia
      October 28, 1805

COLONY: Virginia

EDUCATION: The Temple, London

PROFESSION: Lawyer, Judge

AT YORK TOWN: September 30, 1777–
      December 1777

When Congress was forced to flee from Philadelphia to York Town, transportation was at a premium. Most of the delegates made the journey on horseback. President John Hancock had the luxury of his own coach. Joseph Jones, a delegate from Virginia, traveled in a borrowed carriage belonging to General George Washington.

The first letter written by Jones in York Town had to do with the state and condition of the vehicle in question:

> I have your Phaeton here . . . the bolt that fastens the pole and part of the long reins were lost, some brass nails also gone, and the lining much dirted and in some places, torn. I will get these little matters repaired and have the carriage and harness kept clean and in good order as I can, which is the least I can do for the use.

But the borrowed vehicle was not the only matter Jones discussed with his friend, the Commander-in-Chief. Greatly distressed by the miserable condition of the Virginia militia he had seen on the roads and angered by the generous Tory support among many Pennsylvanians, he strongly advised Washington to help himself to whatever supplies he might find in Tory hands:

> Our friends are stripped by our Enemies wherever they go, and our Foes freely furnish them

what they want . . . I would not scruple to take all necessaries from the disaffected wherever found . . . In pursuing this line, individuals may suffer hardship, but it is a sacrifice our friends should willingly make in the general good. Pray excuse these loose thoughts. I offer them with freedom. You are equally free to disregard them.

Such outspoken advice to his superior indicated some basic relationship between the two Virginians. It also reveals the writer's deep concern for the general welfare.

Joseph Jones, though not a spectacular patriot, was a man of deep conviction and unquestioned integrity. During his rather uneventful career in Congress, his loyalty to Washington never waivered. In January of 1778, when Washington's popularity was waning and his congressional support weakening, Jones took it upon himself to warn his friend of skullduggery in high places:

The conduct and language of a certain popular Pennsylvanian lately appointed to the new Board of War (Thomas Mifflin) of the disposition and Temper of another Gentleman of the Board whose name (General Horatio Gates) the fortunate events of last fall (the surrender of Saratoga) hath greatly exalted. But whatever may be the Design of these men, I have no doubt that, in the end, it will rebound to their own disgrace. You stand too high in public opinion to be easily reached by their conduct. The same labour and attention which you have manifested in the public service from the first contest, will shield and protect you from the shafts of Envy and malevolence.

After resigning from Congress for reasons of health (or a judgeship awaiting him in Virginia), he returned to his home and served his state for the remainder of his life. He was "a confidential friend of President Washington, a correspondent and supporter of Jefferson, an intimate colleague of Madison, and the devoted uncle of James Monroe."

The Silent Partner

FRANCIS LIGHTFOOT LEE

BIRTH: Stratford Hall, Westmoreland County, Virginia
October 14, 1734

DEATH: Richmond County, Virginia
January 11, 1797

COLONY: Virginia

EDUCATION: Private tutors

OCCUPATION: Planter

AT YORK TOWN: September 30, 1777–
May 30, 1778

The excitement that pervaded Stratford Hall on October 14, 1734, when Hannah Ludwell Lee gave birth to her eighth child, was perhaps not as great as that which attended the delivery of her firstborn, but this baby boy was no less welcome. Virginia planters needed sons, not only to manage their estates and to carry on the name but also to bear their share of responsibility for the general welfare of the colony. As Thomas Lee stood in the east bedchamber where, two years before, he had welcomed another son, Richard Henry, into the world, he must have been proud and grateful for the safe arrival of the child destined to uphold the family tradition, with the name of Francis Lightfoot.

By the time that Francis Lightfoot Lee was six years old, two more baby brothers were occupying the nursery—William, born in 1739; and Arthur, born in 1740. But it was Richard Henry who became his playmate and constant companion. From early childhood, Richard was the leader and Francis the follower, a pattern that was to continue throughout their adult lives.

The brothers were first separated when Richard was sent to school in England. Studying at home, Francis was instructed in the Classics, mathematics, and history. His basic schooling, coupled with a first-hand knowledge of plantation affairs and their management, was adequate preparation for life as a Virginia gentleman.

When Richard and Francis were re-united the year after their father's death, the impressionable seventeen-year-old found his older brother a figure to admire and to emulate, even though their individual differences were pronounced. Richard was sophisticated, self-assured, and eloquent. Francis was provincial, shy, and reticent. But, they were also possessed of marked similarities—keen intellects, dedication to public service, and a deep-seated interest in politics.

Francis Lightfoot Lee did not need his brother's rhetoric or the impassioned words of Patrick Henry to convince him about the tyranny of the Stamp Act and the necessity of resistance to any and all measures that violated the rights of freeborn Englishmen. In matters of conscience, he was his own man, and as a Virginian, he firmly believed in the principles of self-government and the importance of the individual. Although he made no defiant speeches in the stormy sessions of the House of Burgesses during the period now known as "The Prelude to Independence," he was, nonetheless, an ardent revolutionist and a true "apostle of change." He was party to every major protest emanating from Williamsburg. Francis, along with his brother Richard, Thomas Jefferson, Dabney Carr, and Patrick Henry, met in the Raleigh Tavern to form the Virginia Committee of Correspondence for closer co-operation with the other colonies.

In 1775, when resistance transformed to revolution, Lee made the transition from the House of Burgesses to the Continental Congress with his customary quiet determination. His brother's famous resolution of June 7, 1776, received his unqualified support. He not only signed the ensuing Declaration of Independence but also served on the committee for drafting the Articles of Confederation.

Lee's four years in Congress, although undistinguished by rhetorical or spectacular leadership, were characterized by integrity and by what one historian has described as "a conscious and sensitive regard for public opinion."

It was this constant regard for the common good that motivated his career and that shaped his decisions. Completely devoid of personal ambition, he neither sought nor received any special honors or recognition. At York Town, he was seriously considered as a successor to the retiring president, John Hancock, but Henry Laurens was elected in his stead.

In 1779, at the age of forty-five, Lee retired from Congress to enjoy the quiet, uncomplicated life of a country gentleman. He devoted himself to the agricultural pursuits afforded by his beloved plantation, Menokin. In the spring of 1797, however, both he and his wife were fatally stricken with pleurisy. The childless couple was buried on the estate where they began their life together—the Taylor plantation of Mount Airy.

Although more pages of history have been devoted to the dynamic leadership of his older brother, Richard Henry, and to the more dramatic exploits of his younger brothers, William and Arthur, the character of Francis Lightfoot Lee typifies the unsung public servant of his day. In a sketch written for the Centennial of 1876, Mark Twain described his life:

[A] good and profitable voyage, though it left no phosphorescent splendors in its wake . . . but the enduring strength of his patriotism was manifest; his fearlessness in confronting perilous duties and encompassing them was patent to all, the purity of his motives was unquestioned, his unpurchasable honor and uprightness were unchallenged . . . let us gravely try to conceive how isolated, how companionless, how lonesome, such a public servant as this would be in Washington today!

A Special Lee

RICHARD HENRY LEE

BORN: Stratford, Westmoreland County,
   Virginia
   January 20, 1732

DIED: Westmoreland County, Virginia
   June 19, 1794

COLONY: Virginia

EDUCATION: Wakefield Academy, England

PROFESSION: Planter, Politician

AT YORK TOWN: September 30, 1777–
   December 1777
   May 1, 1778–
   May 31, 1778

The fifth son of the First Fami-"lee" of Virginia, Richard Henry Lee was "Especial-Lee" true to the Lee tradition of public service and high standards of personal responsibility. By the time he was twenty-five, he had been appointed Justice of the Peace, married Anne Aylette, and established his own home on the estate of "Chantilly," a few miles from his birthplace at Stratford.

When Lee entered the House of Burgesses the following year, he was a rather quiet, reserved young man, somewhat shy and constrained in the presence of his elders. But in his first speech in the House, supporting a measure to check the growth of slavery, his passionate convictions overcame his diffidence and established his reputation as a gifted orator. His reaction to the Stamp Act was yet another demonstration of his hatred of tyranny and oppression of any kind. He is reputed to have led a "mob of gentlemen" against the appointed tax collector, forcing the man to abandon his duties. He was not alone in his actions or his sympathies, being a boon companion of and serving on committees with Patrick Henry, Thomas Jefferson, Peyton Randolph, and George Washington.

Long before the Continental Congress of 1776 addressed the idea of American independence, Richard Henry Lee was convinced that nothing short of absolute political separation would ever succeed in stopping British oppression and misrule.

This conviction was based largely on political intelligence as to the movements and opinions of Parliament relayed to him by his brother, Arthur, who was at that time a distinguished literary figure in London. When Lee attended the Congress of 1776, he was prepared in mind and heart to propose such a move whenever the opportunity arose.

The opportunity did arise on June 7th of that year. Acting from his own conscience and instructions from the Assembly of Virginia, he introduced the following resolution:

> Resolved that these united Colonies are, and of a right, ought to be, free and independent states; that they are absolved from all allegiance to the British Crown; and that all political connection between them and the state of Great Britain is, and ought to be, totally dissolved.

This was, undoubtedly, Lee's finest hour. That hour was cut short by news of his wife's illness, forcing his departure and preventing his appointment to the committee charged with drafting such a Declaration.

In less than a month, the dream of American independence became a reality. But after independence, then what? How and by whom was the new nation to be governed? The answer to that question was contained in the second part of Lee's original resolution; "That a plan of confederation be prepared and submitted to the respective colonies for their consideration."

On July 12, 1776, the Articles of Confederation and Perpetual Union, as drafted by John Dickinson of Pennsylvania, were presented to Congress, and copies were secretly distributed for consideration by individual states. These Articles were the prime business of Congress at York Town from October 3rd until November 15th, when they were finally completed. As each article was debated, hashed, and re-hashed, discussions were long and tempers short. When the delegates were deadlocked over the basis of taxation, it was the wise counsel of Richard Henry Lee that finally prevailed:

> I must note that in this great business of forming our first common charter, we must yield a little to each other, and no rigidity insist on having everything correspond to our partial views. On such basis we would NEVER be able to confederate.

Richard Henry Lee had the satisfaction of signing both the Declaration of Independence and the Articles of Confederation, which were completed after fifteen months of careful deliberation. Although not perfect, these articles were, in fact, the first constitutional government of the New World, thereby making the Court House of York County the first Capitol of the United States.

Other matters beside the Articles also claimed the attention of Mr. Lee of Virginia. One was the urgent need of a printing press. As Chairman of the Committee of Intelligence, Lee wrote the order to Hall and Sellers, the Philadelphia printing firm that had managed to move their press (once the property of Ben Franklin) to Lancaster for safe-keeping. The presses eventually arrived, but not in time to print the Articles, which were published by Francis Bailey of Lancaster. However, the Hall and Sellers press was installed in time to print the first Thanksgiving proclamation, however, as well as the terms of the Saratoga Convention. The *Pennsylvania Gazette* was also printed in York Town from December 20, 1777, to June 20, 1778.

Lee continued to serve his country during times of peace as well as war. Like many other revolutionary patriots, he was opposed to the Constitution, but when it was ratified, he served as the first Virginia senator under the new regime. Failing health finally forced his retirement from public life.

Richard Henry was "A Special Lee" in many different ways. He was "Especial-Lee" gifted in intelligence, oratory, and leadership. He will also long be remembered as an aristocrat who was foremost in breaking down distinctions between the wealthy class and the "common people," a label coined by the aristocracy for those who labored with their hands.

THE ARTICLES OF CONFEDERATION

AGREED TO BY CONGRESS ON NOVEMBER 15, 1777; RATIFIED AND IN FORCE ON MARCH 1, 1781.

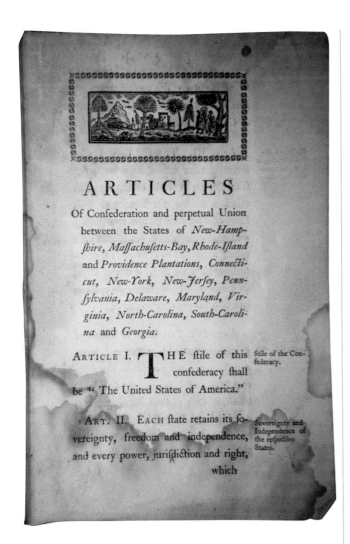

PREAMBLE

To all to whom these Presents shall come, we the undersigned Delegates of the States affixed to our Names send greeting. Whereas the Delegates of the United States of America in Congress assembled did on the fifteenth day of November in the Year of our Lord One Thousand Seven Hundred and Seventy Seven, and in the Second Year of the Independence of America agree to certain articles of Confederation and perpetual Union between the States of New Hampshire, Massachusetts bay, Rhode Island and Providence Plantations, Connecticut, New York, New Jersey, Pennsylvania, Delaware, Maryland, Virginia, North Carolina, South Carolina and Georgia in the Words following, viz. "Articles of Confederation and perpetual Union between the States of New Hampshire, Massachusetts bay, Rhode Island and Providence Plantations, Connecticut, New York, New Jersey, Pennsylvania, Delaware, Maryland, Virginia, North Carolina, South Carolina and Georgia."

ARTICLE I

The Stile of this Confederacy shall be "The United States of America."

ARTICLE II

Each state retains its sovereignty, freedom, and independence, and every power, jurisdiction, and right, which is not by this Confederation expressly delegated to the United States, in Congress assembled.

ARTICLE III

The said States hereby severally enter into a firm league of friendship with each other, for their common defense, the security of their liberties, and their mutual and general welfare, binding themselves to assist each other, against all force offered to, or attacks made upon them, or any of them, on account of religion, sovereignty, trade, or any other pretense whatever.

ARTICLE IV

The better to secure and perpetuate mutual friendship and intercourse among the people of the different States in this Union, the free inhabitants of each of these States, paupers, vagabonds, and fugitives from justice excepted, shall be entitled to all privileges and immunities of free citizens in the several States; and the people of each State shall free ingress and regress to and from any other State, and shall enjoy therein all the privileges of trade and commerce, subject to the same duties, impositions, and restrictions as the inhabitants thereof respectively, provided that such restrictions shall not extend so far as to prevent the removal of property imported into any State, to any other State, of which the owner is an inhabitant; provided also that no imposition, duties or restriction shall be laid by any State, on the property of the United States, or either of them.

If any person guilty of, or charged with, treason, felony, or other high misdemeanor in any State, shall flee from justice, and be found in any of the United States, he shall, upon demand of the Governor or executive power of the State from which he fled, be delivered up and removed to the State having jurisdiction of his offense.

Full faith and credit shall be given in each of these States to the records, acts, and judicial proceedings of the courts and magistrates of every other State.

ARTICLE V

For the most convenient management of the general interests of the United States, delegates shall be annually appointed in such manner as the legislatures of each State shall direct, to meet in Congress on the first Monday in November, in every year, with a power reserved to each State to recall its delegates, or any of them, at any time within the year, and to send others in their stead for the remainder of the year.

No State shall be represented in Congress by less than two, nor more than seven members; and no person shall be capable of being a delegate for more than three years in any term of six years; nor shall any person, being a delegate, be capable of holding any office under the United States, for which he, or another for his benefit, receives any salary, fees or emolument of any kind.

Each State shall maintain its own delegates in a meeting of the States, and while they act as members of the committee of the States.

In determining questions in the United States in Congress assembled, each State shall have one vote.

Freedom of speech and debate in Congress shall not be impeached or questioned in any court or place out of Congress, and the members of Congress shall be protected in their persons from arrests or imprisonments, during the time of their going to and from, and attendance on Congress, except for treason, felony, or breach of the peace.

ARTICLE VI

No State, without the consent of the United States in Congress assembled, shall send any embassy to, or receive any embassy from, or enter into any conference, agreement, alliance or treaty with any King, Prince or State; nor shall any person holding any office of profit or trust under the United States, or any of them, accept any present, emolument, office or title of any kind whatever from any King, Prince or foreign State; nor shall the United States in Congress assembled, or any of them, grant any title of nobility.

No two or more States shall enter into any treaty, confederation or alliance whatever between them, without the consent of the United States in Congress assembled, specifying accurately the purposes for which the same is to be entered into, and how long it shall continue.

No State shall lay any imposts or duties, which may interfere with any stipulations in treaties, entered into by the United States in Congress assembled, with any King, Prince or State, in pursuance of any treaties already proposed by Congress, to the courts of France and Spain.

No vessel of war shall be kept up in time of peace by any State, except such number only, as shall be deemed necessary by the United States in Congress assembled, for the defense of such State, or its trade; nor shall any body of forces be kept up by any State in time of peace, except such number only, as in the judgement of the United States in Congress assembled, shall be deemed requisite to garrison the forts necessary for the defense of such State; but every State shall always keep up a well-regulated and disciplined militia, sufficiently armed and accoutered, and shall provide and constantly have ready for use, in public stores, a due number of field pieces and tents, and a proper quantity of arms, ammunition and camp equipage.

No State shall engage in any war without the consent of the United States in Congress assembled, unless such State be actually invaded by enemies, or shall have received certain advice of a resolution being formed by some nation of Indians to invade such State, and the danger is so imminent as not to admit of a delay till the United States in Congress assembled can be consulted; nor shall any State grant commissions to any ships or vessels of war, nor letters of marque or reprisal, except it be after a declaration of war by the United States in Congress assembled, and then only against the

Kingdom or State and the subjects thereof, against which war has been so declared, and under such regulations as shall be established by the United States in Congress assembled, unless such State be infested by pirates, in which case vessels of war may be fitted out for that occasion, and kept so long as the danger shall continue, or until the United States in Congress assembled shall determine otherwise.

ARTICLE VII

When land forces are raised by any State for the common defense, all officers of or under the rank of colonel, shall be appointed by the legislature of each State respectively, by whom such forces shall be raised, or in such manner as such State shall direct, and all vacancies shall be filled up by the State which first made the appointment.

ARTICLE VIII

All charges of war, and all other expenses that shall be incurred for the common defense or general welfare, and allowed by the United States in Congress assembled, shall be defrayed out of a common treasury, which shall be supplied by the several States in proportion to the value of all land within each State, granted or surveyed for any person, as such land and the buildings and improvements thereon shall be estimated according to such mode as the United States in Congress assembled, shall from time to time direct and appoint.

The taxes for paying that proportion shall be laid and levied by the authority and direction of the legislatures of the several States within the time agreed upon by the United States in Congress assembled.

ARTICLE IX

The United States in Congress assembled, shall have the sole and exclusive right and power of determining on peace and war, except in the cases mentioned in the sixth article—of sending and receiving ambassadors—entering into treaties and alliances, provided that no treaty of commerce shall be made whereby the legislative power of the respective States shall be restrained from imposing such imposts and duties on foreigners, as their own people are subjected to, or from prohibiting the exportation or importation of any species of goods or commodities whatsoever—of establishing rules for deciding in all cases, what captures on land or water shall be legal, and in what manner prizes taken by land or naval forces in the service of the United States shall be divided or appropriated—of granting letters of marque and reprisal in times of peace—appointing courts for the trial of piracies and felonies committed on the high seas and establishing courts for receiving and determining finally appeals in all cases of captures, provided that no member of Congress shall be appointed a judge of any of the said courts.

The United States in Congress assembled shall also be the last resort on appeal in all disputes and differences now subsisting or that hereafter may arise between two or more States concerning boundary, jurisdiction or any other causes whatever; which authority shall always be exercised in the manner following. Whenever the legislative or executive authority or lawful agent of any State in controversy with another shall present a petition to Congress stating the matter in question and praying for a hearing, notice thereof shall be given by order of Congress to the legislative or executive authority of the other State in controversy, and a day assigned for the appearance of the parties by their lawful agents, who shall then be directed to appoint by joint consent, commissioners or judges to constitute a court for hearing and determining the matter in question: but if they cannot agree, Congress shall name three persons out of each of the United States, and from the list of such persons each party shall alternately strike out one, the petitioners beginning, until the number shall be reduced to thirteen; and from that number not less than seven, nor more than nine names as Congress shall direct, shall in the presence of Congress be drawn out by lot, and the persons whose names shall be so drawn or any five of them, shall be commissioners or judges, to hear and finally determine the controversy, so always as a major part of the judges who shall hear the cause shall agree in the determination: and if either party shall neglect to attend at the day appointed, without showing reasons, which Congress shall judge sufficient, or being present shall refuse to strike, the Congress shall proceed to nominate three persons out of each State, and the secretary of Congress shall strike in behalf of such party absent or refusing; and the judgement and sentence of the court to be appointed, in the manner before prescribed, shall be final and conclusive; and if any of the parties shall refuse to submit to the authority of such court, or to appear or defend their claim or cause, the court shall nevertheless proceed to pronounce sentence, or judgement, which shall in like manner be final and decisive, the judgement or sentence and other proceedings being in either case transmitted to Congress, and lodged among the acts of Congress for the security of the parties concerned: provided that every commissioner, before he sits in judgement, shall take an oath to be administered by one of the judges of the supreme or superior court of the State, where the cause shall be tried, 'well and truly to hear and determine the matter in question, according to the best of his judgement, without favor, affection or hope of reward': provided also, that no State shall be deprived of territory for the benefit of the United States.

All controversies concerning the private right of soil claimed under different grants of two or more States, whose jurisdictions as they may respect such lands, and the States which passed such grants are adjusted, the said grants or either of them being at the same time claimed to have originated antecedent to such settlement of jurisdiction, shall on the petition of either party to the Congress of the United States, be finally determined as near as may be in the same manner as is before prescribed for deciding disputes respecting territorial jurisdiction between different States.

The United States in Congress assembled shall also have the sole and exclusive right and power of regulating the alloy and value of coin struck by their own authority, or by that of the respective States—fixing the standards of weights and measures throughout the United States—regulating the trade and managing all affairs with the Indians, not members of any of the States, provided that the legislative right of any State within its own limits be not infringed or violated—establishing or regulating post offices from one State to another, throughout all the United States, and exacting such postage on the papers passing through the same as may be requisite to defray the expenses of the said office—appointing all officers of the land forces, in the service of the United States, excepting regimental officers—appointing all the officers of the naval forces, and commissioning all officers whatever in the service of the United States — making rules for the government and regulation of the said land and naval forces, and directing their operations.

The United States in Congress assembled shall have authority to appoint a committee, to sit in the recess of Congress, to be denominated 'A Committee of the States', and to consist of one delegate from each State; and to appoint such other committees and civil officers as may be necessary for managing the general affairs of the United States under their direction—to appoint one of their members to preside, provided that no person be allowed to serve in the office of president more than one year in any term of three years; to ascertain the necessary sums of money to be raised for the service of the United States, and to appropriate and apply the same for defraying the public expenses—to borrow money, or emit bills on the credit of the United States, transmitting every half-year to the respective States an account of the sums of money so borrowed or emitted—to build and equip a navy—to agree upon the number of land forces, and to make requisitions from each State for its quota, in proportion to the number of white inhabitants in such State; which requisition shall be binding, and thereupon the legislature of each State shall appoint the regimental officers, raise the men and cloath, arm and equip them in a solid-like manner, at the expense of the United States; and the officers and men so cloathed, armed and equipped shall march to the place appointed, and within the time agreed on by the United States in Congress assembled. But if the United States in Congress assembled shall, on consideration of circumstances judge proper that any State should not raise men, or should raise a smaller number of men than the quota thereof, such extra number shall be raised, officered, cloathed, armed and equipped in the same manner as the quota of each State, unless the legislature of such State shall judge that such extra number cannot be safely spread out in the same, in which case they shall raise, officer, cloath, arm and equip as many of such extra number as they judge can be safely spared. And the officers and men so cloathed, armed, and equipped, shall march to the place appointed, and within the time agreed on by the United States in Congress assembled.

The United States in Congress assembled shall never engage in a war, nor grant letters of marque or reprisal in time of peace, nor enter into any treaties or alliances, nor coin money, nor regulate the value thereof, nor ascertain the sums and expenses necessary for the defense and welfare of the United States, or any of them, nor emit bills, nor borrow money on the credit of the United States, nor appropriate money, nor agree upon the number of vessels of war, to be built or purchased, or the number of land or sea forces to be raised, nor appoint a commander in chief of the army or navy, unless nine States assent to the same: nor shall a question on any other point, except for adjourning from day to day be determined, unless by the votes of the majority of the United States in Congress assembled.

The Congress of the United States shall have power to adjourn to any time within the year, and to any place within the United States, so that no period of adjournment be for a longer duration than the space of six months, and shall publish the journal of their proceedings monthly, except such parts thereof relating to treaties, alliances or military operations, as in their judgement require secrecy; and the yeas and nays of the delegates of each State on any question shall be entered on the journal, when it is desired by any delegates of a State, or any of them, at his or their request shall be furnished with a transcript of the said journal, except such parts as are above excepted, to lay before the legislatures of the several States.

ARTICLE X

The Committee of the States, or any nine of them, shall be authorized to execute, in the recess of Congress, such of the powers of Congress as the United States in Congress assembled, by the consent of the nine States, shall from time to time think expedient to vest them with; provided that no power be delegated to the said Committee, for the exercise of which, by the Articles of Confederation, the voice of nine States in the Congress of the United States assembled be requisite.

ARTICLE XI

Canada acceding to this confederation, and adjoining in the measures of the United States, shall be admitted into, and entitled to all the advantages of this Union; but no other colony shall be admitted into the same, unless such admission be agreed to by nine States.

ARTICLE XII

All bills of credit emitted, monies borrowed, and debts contracted by, or under the authority of Congress, before the assembling of the United States, in pursuance of the present confederation, shall be deemed and considered as a charge against the United States, for payment and satisfaction whereof the said United States, and the public faith are hereby solemnly pledged.

ARTICLE XIII

Every State shall abide by the determination of the United States in Congress assembled, on all questions which by this confederation are submitted to them. And the Articles of this Confederation shall be inviolably observed by every State, and the Union shall be perpetual; nor shall any alteration at any time hereafter be made in any of them; unless such alteration be agreed to in a Congress of the United States, and be afterwards confirmed by the legislatures of every State.

And Whereas it hath pleased the Great Governor of the World to incline the hearts of the legislatures we respectively represent in Congress, to approve of, and to authorize us to ratify the said Articles of Confederation and perpetual Union. Know Ye that we the undersigned delegates, by virtue of the power and authority to us given for that purpose, do by these presents, in the name and in behalf of our respective constituents, fully and entirely ratify and confirm each and every of the said Articles of Confederation and perpetual Union, and all and singular the matters and things therein contained: And we do further solemnly plight and engage the faith of our respective constituents, that they shall abide by the determinations of the United States in Congress assembled, on all questions, which by the said Confederation are submitted to them. And that the Articles thereof shall be inviolably observed by the States we respectively represent, and that the Union shall be perpetual.

In Witness whereof we have hereunto set our hands in Congress. Done at Philadelphia in the State of Pennsylvania the ninth day of July in the Year of our Lord One Thousand Seven Hundred and Seventy-Eight, and in the Third Year of the independence of America.

On the part and behalf of the State of New Hampshire:
  Josiah Bartlett
  John Wentworth Junr.
  August 8th 1778

On the part and behalf of the State of Massachusetts Bay:
  John Hancock
  Francis Dana
  Samuel Adams
  James Lovell
  Elbridge Gerry
  Samuel Holten

On the part and behalf of the State of Rhode Island and Providence Plantations:
  William Ellery
  John Collins
  Henry Marchant

On the part and behalf of the State of Connecticut:
  Roger Sherman
  Titus Hosmer
  Samuel Huntington
  Andrew Adams
  Oliver Wolcott

On the Part and Behalf of the State of New York:
    James Duane
    Wm Duer
    Francis Lewis
    Gouv Morris

On the Part and in Behalf of the State of New Jersey, November 26, 1778:
    Jno Witherspoon
    Nathaniel Scudder

On the part and behalf of the State of Pennsylvania:
    Robt Morris
    William Clingan
    Daniel Roberdeau
    Joseph Reed
    John Bayard Smith
    22nd July 1778

On the part and behalf of the State of Delaware:
    Tho Mckean February 12, 1779
    John Dickinson May 5th 1779
    Nicholas Van Dyke

On the part and behalf of the State of Maryland:
    John Hanson March 1 1781
    Daniel Carroll Do

On the Part and Behalf of the State of Virginia:
    Richard Henry Lee
    Jno Harvie
    John Banister
    Francis Lightfoot Lee
    Thomas Adams

On the part and Behalf of the State of No Carolina:
    John Penn July 21st 1778
    Corns Harnett
    Jno Williams

On the part and behalf of the State of South Carolina:
    Henry Laurens
    Richd Hutson
    William Henry Drayton
    Thos Heyward Junr
    Jno Mathews

On the part and behalf of the State of Georgia:
    Jno Walton 24th July 1778
    Edwd Telfair
    Edwd Langworthy

BIBLIOGRAPHIC NOTES

Although not a comprehensive list, the sources cited here may be of benefit to readers wishing to understand the research process of John F. Rauhauser, Jr., and as a guide to those wanting more detailed information about the delegates' lives. While the biographies of certain delegates have been thoroughly assembled, for others, that task remains unfulfilled. The sources most relied upon to compile these life sketches were the *Biographical Directory of the American Congress*, Lossing's *Biographical Sketches of the Signers of the Declaration of Independence*, and Marshall's *The United States Manual of Biography and History*. Many of the sketches' direct quotations were drawn from Burnett's *Letters of Members of the Continental Congress* and Smith's *Letters of Delegates to Congress*.

Generally speaking, the holdings of both the National Archives and the Library of Congress contain significant materials: so, respectively, do the various state archives. Many local historical societies would also prove useful for more detailed research, as would repositories of primary sources such as state and county governmental offices.

These bibliographic sources are divided as two components: those that are comprehensive in nature and those pertaining to specific delegates.

GENERAL BIBLIOGRAPHIC REFERENCES

Appleton's Cyclopaedia of American Biography (1894–1900) (**ACAB**)

Bakeless, John and Katherine. *Signers of the Declaration* (1969)

Biographical Directory of the American Congress, 1774–1989 (1989) (**BDAC**)

Boatner, Mark Mayo, ed. *Encyclopedia of the American Revolution* (c. 1979) (**EAR**)

Burnett, Edmond Cody, ed. *Letters of Members of the Continental Congress (1921–1936)* (**LMCC**)

Volume II July 3, 1776 to December 31, 1777

Volume III January 1, 1778 to December 31, 1778

Carnegie Institution of Washington, Publication No. 297

Coleman, John. *Thomas McKean, Forgotten Leader of the Revolution* (1975)

Fairhurst, Janet. *Homes of the Signers of the Declaration* (1976)

Ford, Chauncy, ed. *Journals of the Continental Congress,* Edited from Original Records in the Library of Congress (1905)

Gotwalt, Helen Miller. *Crucible of a New Nation* (1977)

Hoffert, Robert W. *A Politics of Tension: The Articles of Confederation and American Political Ideas* (c. 1992)

Jensen, Merrill. *The Articles of Confederation: An Interpretation of the Social-Conditional History of the American Revolution, 1774–1781* (1966) (**AOC**)

Journals of the Continental Congress. Vols I–XVIII. Edited from the original records in Library of Congress by Wiorthington Chauncy Ford (1905)

Lossing, Benson, J. *Biographical Sketches of the Signers of the Declaration of Independence* (1860) (**BSS**)

The American Historical Record, and Repertory of Notes and Queries Concerning the History and Antiquities of America and Biography of Americans (1872)

Malone, Dumas, ed. *Dictionary of American Biography* (1932) (**DAB**)

Marshall, James V. *The United States Manual of Biography and History* (1856) (**MBH**)

Moore, Frank. *Diary of the Revolution* (1876) (**DR**)

Movers, Frank C., ed. *The Papers of Josiah Bartlett* (1979)

National Archives and Records Administration

Drafts of Articles, Record of Proceedings of Second Continental Congress Relating to the Adoption and Ratification of the Articles; and Proposals on Locating the Seat of Government and Printing the Journals, 1777–1789

Index to the Journals of the Continental Congress, 1774–1789

Index to the Papers of the Continental Congress, 1774–1789

Records Relating to Congressional Activities: General Index to the Records of the Confederation Congress, 1781–1789

National Encyclopedia of American Biography (1893–1984) (**NCAB**)

National Park Service, Independence Hall, *Philadelphia Signers of the Declaration: Biographical Sketches* (n.d.) (**NPS**)

Sanderson, John, ed. *Biographies of the Signers of the Declaration of Independence (1823–1827)* (**BSDI**)

Smith, Paul H., ed. *Letters of Delegates to Congress* (1976) (**LDC**)

Vennis, J. A. *Alumni Cantabridgiensis, Part II: 1752–1900.* Vol. IV, K-O

Walthe, Daniel. *Gouverneur Morris, Witness of Two Revolutions*, Trans. Elinore Denniston (1934)

Witney, David C. *Founders of Freedom in America* (1964)

USEFUL WEBSITES

www.Abebooks.com

Biographical Dictionary of the United States Congress, 1774–Present (**BCG**)
bioguide.congress.gov

Colonial Hall (**CH**)
www.colonialhall.com

www.FindAGrave.com

National Archives and Record Administration
www.nara.gov/nail.html

The Political Graveyard: Index to Politicians (**PG**)
politicalgraveyard.com

www.YorkLibraries.org

BIOGRAPHICAL SOURCES PERTAINING TO SPECIFIC DELEGATES

Adams, J.
AOC, BSS, DR, NCAB, NPS

Adams, S.
AOC, BSS, DR, LMCC
Hosmer, James K. *Samuel Adams* (1885)

Adams, T.
BCG, PG
Daniel, Frederick. "Some Colonial and Revolutionary Letters," *Harper's Magazine*, July, 1890
Miller, Florence Hazen. *Memorial Album of Revolutionary Soldiers, 1776* (1958)
Tarter, Brent. "Richard Adams and Thomas Adams of New Kent County and Richmond," *The Richmond Quarterly*, 1989
Waddell, Joseph A. *Annals of Augusta County, Virginia, from 1726 to 1871* (1902)

Bannister, J.
BDAC
Horner, Frederick. *The History of the Blair, Banister, and Braxton Families Before and After the Revolution* (1898)

Bartlett, J.
BDAC, BSS, CH
The Papers of Josiah Bartlett (c. 1979)

Brownson, N.
LMCC
Candler, Allen D., ed. *The Revolutionary Records of the State of Georgia* (1908)
Coleman, Kenneth. *The American Revolution in Georgia, 1763–1789* (1958)
Jones, Jr., Charles C. *Biographical Sketches of the Delegates from Georgia to the Continental Congress* (1891)
"The Constitution in Georgia," *Georgia Historical Quarterly*, Vol. 58
"The Puritan in Georgia," *Georgia Historical Quarterly*, Vol. 13

Burke, T.
BDAC, LMCC

Carroll, C.
AOC, BSS, DR, LMCC, NPS
Andrews, Matthew Page. *Tercentenary History of Maryland* (1925)
Smith, Ellen Hart. *Charles Carroll of Carrollton* (1942)

Chase, S.
AOC, BSS, LMCC
Andrews, Matthew Page. *Tercentenary History of Maryland* (1925)

Clark, A.
    BCG

Clingan, W.
    BCG, CH, LMCC
    Cope, Gilbert. *History of Chester County,*
      Pennsylvania (1881)

Collins, L.
    ACAB, BCG, CH, MBH
    Biographical Cyclopaedia of Representative
      Men of Rhode Island (1881)

Dana, F.
    LMCC, NCAB
    Cresson, W. P. *Francis Dana, a Puritan*
      Diplomat

Drayton, W.
    BSS
    O'Neall, J. B. *Biographical Sketch of the*
      Bench and Bar of South Carolina (1859)

Duane, J.
    AOC, DR, LMCC

Duer, W.
    AOC, DAB, DR, EAR, LMCC
    Jones, Thomas. *History of New York During*
      the Revolutionary War (1879)

Dyer, E.
    AOC, DR, LMCC, NCAB

Ellery, W.
    BSS, LMCC, NPS

Elmer, J.
    BCG, DR, LMCC
    Chestnut, Bill. "The World of Bridge Town's
      U. S. Senator, Jonathan Elmer," *South*
      Jersey Magazine, Winter, 1989
    Inner City Archives and Records Center,
      University of Pennsylvania, Philadelphia, PA
      19104-6320 (medical diploma)
    Rogers, Fred B. "Jonathan Elmer: Medical
      Progenitor," *Journal of the Medical Society*
      of New Jersey, April, 1976

Folsom, N.
    LMCC
    (Also papers collected in the Library of
      Congress)

Forbes, J.
    BCG, PG

Biographical Dictionary of the Maryland
    Legislature, 1635–1789 (1979)

Frost, G.
    LMCC
    Farmer, J., and J. B. Moore, eds. *Collections,*
      Historical and Miscellaneous: and Monthly
      Literary Journal. Vol. II (1823)
    Frost, John Eldridge. *The Nicholas Frost*
      Family (1943)
    The New England Historical and Genealogical
      Register, Vol. CIV (1950)
    Stackpole, Everett S. and Lucien Thompson,
      History of the Town of Durham, New
      Hampshire, Vol. I (n.d.)

Gerry, E.
    AOC, BSS, LMCC, NCAB
    Library of Congress. *Elbridge Gerry Papers,*
      MS Group 297, 8 boxes, 2 vols.

Hancock, J.
    BSS, LMCC
    Adams, James T. "Portrait of an Empty Barrel,"
      Harper's Magazine, September, 1930
    Allan, Herbert S. *John Hancock: Patriot in*
      Purple (1949)
    Wagner, Frederick. *Peoples' Choice: The Story*
      of John Hancock (1964)

Harnett, C.
    AOC, LMCC
    Morgan, David T. "Cornelius Harnett:
      Revolutionary Leader and Delegate to the
      Continental Congress," *The North Carolina*
      Historical Review, Vol. XLIX, No. 3, July,
      1972
    Swain, David Lowry. "Life and Letters of
      Cornelius Harnett," *North Carolina*
      University Magazine, Vol. X, No. 6,
      February, 1861
    Watson, Alan D. *Cornelius Harnett* (1979)

Harrison, B.
    AOC, BSS, LMCC

Harvie, J.
    BDAC, LMCC

Henry, Jr., J.
    Andrews, Matthew Page. *Tercentenary History*
      of Maryland (1925)

Heyward, T.
    BSS, CH, LMCC, NPS

Edgar, Walter B. and N. Louise Bailey. *Biographical Directory of the South Carolina House of Representatives,* Vol. II.

Holten, S.
LMCC
Holten Manuscript Collection, Danvers Historical Society, Danvers, Massachusetts

Hosmer, T.
BCG, CH
Dexter, Frank B. *Biographical Sketches of the Graduates of Yale College, 1885–1912* (1912)
Hinman, R.R. *An Historical Collection from Official Records, Files, Etc., of the Part Sustained by Connecticut During the War of the Revolution* (1836)
Hosmer Files, Hartford County, Connecticut, Historical Society

Huntington, S.
Van Dusen, Albert E. "Samuel Huntington: A Leader of Revolutionary Connecticut," *Connecticut Historical Society Bulletin,* Vol. 19, No. 2, April, 1954

Hutson, R.
Hutson, William Mains. "The Hutson Family of South Carolina," *South Carolina Historical and Genealogical Magazine,* Vol. 9, 1908
McLachlan, James. *Princetonians, 1746–1768* (1976)
O'Neall, John Belton. *Biographical Sketches of the Bench and Bar of South Carolina* (1859)
"Letters of the Honorable Richard Hutson," *Yearbook of the City of Charleston, South Carolina* (1895)

Jones, J.
AOC, BCG, LMCC
Letters of Joseph Jones of Virginia, Government Printing Office, Washington, D.C. (1889)
McAllister, Major Howard Landon. Paper on Judge Joseph Jones (c1970s), original work is housed at James Monroe Museum and Memorial Library, 908 Charles Street, Fredericksburg, VA 22401

Langworthy, E.
Burnett, Edmund C. "Edward Langworthy in the Continental Congress," *The Georgia Historical Quarterly,* Vol. XII, No. 3, September, 1928

Perkins, Eunice Ross. "The Progress of the Revolution," *Georgian Historical Quarterly,* Vol. 31 (n.d.)

Laurens, H.
AOC, BSS, DR, LMCC

Law, R.
AOC, DAB, LMCC, NCAB
Dexter, Franklin B. *Biographical Sketches of the Graduates of Yale College, 1885–1912* (1912)
Dictionary of American Biographies, Vol 6 (c. 1933)

Lee. F.
BDAC, BSDI, BSS, LMCC

Lee, R.
AOC, BDAC, BSS, DR, LMCC

Lewis, F.
BCG, CH, PG

Livingston, P.
BCG, CH, PG

Lovell, J.
Shipton, Clifford K. *Biographical Sketches of Those Who Attended Harvard College in the Classes 1756–1760, Sibley's Harvard Graduates* (1968)

McKean, T.
BSS
Colman, John M. *Thomas McKean, Forgotten Leader of the Revolution* (1975)
Frazier, Caxton. "Unknown Signers of the Declaration," *The Mentor* (n.d.)

Marchant, H.
ACAB, BCG, CH, PG

Mathewes, J.
CH, MBH
Edgar, Walter B. and N. Louise Bailey. *Biographical Dictionary of the South Carolina House of Representatives* (1974)

Middleton, A.
BCG, BDAC, BSS
Cheves, Langdon. "Middleton of South Carolina," *The South Carolina Historical and Genealogical Magazine,* Vol. I, No. 3, July, 1900

"Correspondence of the Honorable Arthur Middleton," *The South Carolina Historical and Genealogical Magazine,* Vol. XXVII, No. 3, July, 1926

Morris, G.
  BSS
  Sparks, Jared. *Life of Gouverneur Morris* (1832)
  Walther, Daniel. *Gouverneur Morris: Witness to Two Revolutions* (1934)

Morris, R.
  AOC, BSS, LMCC, NCAB

Penn, J.
  AOC, BCG, BSS, CH, LMCC, NPS
  Kingsbury, Theodore B. "John Penn of Granville," *Wake Forest Historical Society Papers* (1899)

Plater, G.
  BCG
  Andrews, Matthew Page. *Tercentenary History of Maryland* (1925)
  Buchholz, H. E. *Governors of Maryland* (1908)
  Swann, Jr., Don. *Colonial and Historic Homes of Maryland* (1975)

Reed, J.
  BCG, CH, EAR, MBH, NCAB

Roberdeau, D.
  ACAB, BCG, CH, LMCC
  Educate the U.S.A.: Biography of Daniel Roberdeau
  http://www.unitedstates-on-line.com

Rumsey, B.
  LMCC
  Biographical Dictionary of the Maryland Legislature, 1635–1789 (1979)

Scudder, N.
  BCG, CH, PG

Sherman, R.
  BCG, CH, PG

Smith, J.
  BCG, BSS, CH
  Gibson, John. *History of York County, Pennsylvania* (1886)
  Orwig, Angela B. *Colonel James Smith: York Town's Very Own Founding Father* (1998)
  "Letters of John Smith," *York County Historical Society Yearbook* (1940)

Smith, J. Bayard
  AOC, BCG
  National Encyclopedia of Biographies, Vol. 6 (c.1933)

Smith, W.
  AOC, LMCC

Walton, G.
  BCG, BSS, NPS
  Bridges, Edwin C. "George Walton: A Political Biography," Ph.D. Dissertation, University of Chicago, 1981

Wentworth, J.
  Bell, Charles H. *The Bench and Bar of New Hampshire* (1894)
  Hurd, D. Hamilton. *History of Rockingham and Strafford Counties, New Hampshire* (1882)
  Shipton, Clifford K. *Sibley's Harvard Graduates, Vol. XVII, 1768–1771* (1975)
  Stearns, Ezra S. *Genealogical and Family History of the State of New Hampshire,* Vol. III (1908)
  Wentworth, John. *The Wentworth Genealogy: English and American,* Vol. II (1878)

Williams, W.
  BSS, LMCC

Witherspoon, J.
  AOC, BSS, DR, LMCC

Wolcott, O.
  Dexter, Franklin B. *Biographical Sketches of the Graduates of Yale College, 1895–1912* (1912)

Wood, J.
  BCG, DR, LMCC, PG

PHOTO AND IMAGE CREDITS

Connecticut; Huntington—National Park Service, Independence Hall; Sherman—National Park Service, Independence Hall; Williams—National Park Service, Inde-pendence Hall; Wolcott—National Park Service, Independence Hall.

Delaware; McKean—National Park Service, Independence Hall.

Georgia; Brownson—Painting by George Mandus (c. 1960s). Courtesy of the Georgia Department of Archives and History; Walton—National Park Service, Independence Hall.

Maryland; Carroll—National Park Service, Independence Hall; Chase—National Park Service, Independence Hall; Platter—From Lossing's Biographical Sketches of the Signers of the Declaration of Independence; William Smith—Courtesy of the Maryland Historical Society, Baltimore, Maryland.

Massachusetts; Adams, J.—National Park Service, Independence Hall; Adams, S.—National Park Service, Independence Hall; Dana—State Library, Boston, Massachusetts; Gerry—National Park Service, Independence Hall; Hancock—National Park Service, Independence Hall; Holten—Courtesy of the Danvers Archival Center, Peabody Institute Library, Danvers, Massachusetts.

New Hampshire; Bartlett—National Park Service, Independence Hall.

New Jersey; Clark—National Park Service, Independence Hall; Elmer—Copy of diploma courtesy of The University of Pennsylvania Archives.

New York; Duane—Lossing's Biographical Sketches of the Signers of the Declaration of Independence; Duer—Lossing's Biographical Sketches of the Signers of the Declaration of Independence; Lewis—National Park Service, Independence Hall; Livingston—Lossing's Biographical Sketches of the Signers of the Declaration of Independence; Morris—National Park Service, Independence Hall.

North Carolina; Penn—National Park Service, Independence Hall.

Pennsylvania; Clingan— Morris—National Park Service, Independence Hall; Reed—National Park Service, Independence Hall; James Smith—Courtesy of The Historical Society of York County, Pennsylvania; Jonathan Bayard Smith—National Park Service, Independence Hall.

Rhode Island; Ellery—National Park Service, Independence Hall.

South Carolina; Drayton—Lossing's Biographical Sketches of the Signers of the Declaration of Independence; Heyward—National Park Service, Independence Hall; Hutson—Painting by James Earle, from the Collection of City Hall, Charleston, South Carolina; Laurens—National Park Service, Independence Hall; Middleton—Courtesy, Middleton Place Foundation, Charleston, SC; National Park Service, Independence Hall.

Virginia; Harrison—National Park Service, Independence Hall; Joseph Jones—Courtesy of the Virginia Historical Society, Richmond, Virginia, and the Valentine Museum, Richmond, Virginia; Francis Lightfoot Lee—National Park Service, Independence Hall; Richard Henry Lee—National Park Service, Independence Hall; Harvie—Courtesy of the Valentine Museum, Richmond, Virginia; Monroe—Image on ivory from James Monroe Museum and Memorial Library, c. 1780s–1800, artist unknown.

SUBJECT INDEX

NAME INDEX

N

North, Frederick (Lord North), 29, 54, 66, 128

P

Paine, Robert Treat, 58
Paine, Thomas, 62
Palfrey, William, 26
Peace proposals of British commissioners, 62
Pendleton, Edmund, 101
Penn, John, 101–102, 160, x
Penn, Moses, 101
Penn, Richard, x
Penn, Susan, 102
Penn, Thomas, x
Penn, William, 110, ix
Pepperell, William, 69
Pettingall, Amy. *See* Lewis, Amy
Plater, Elizabeth (Rousby), 42
Plater, George, 41–42
Plater, Hannah (Lee), 42
Plater, Thomas, 41, 42
Pope, Alexander, 100
Prentise, Ann. *See* Law, Ann
Prescott, Rebecca. *See* Sherman, Rebecca
Price, Jonathan, 59
Price, Mary (Warner), 59

Q

Quincy, Dolly. *See* Hancock, Dolly
Quincy, John, 99

R

Randolph, Anne Carey (Nancy). *See* Morris, Anne Carey
Randolph, Peyton, 58, 144, 153
Read, George, 20
Reed, Esther (DeBerdt), 108
Reed, John, 68
Reed, Joseph, 109–110, 160
Revere, Paul, 51
Richard III, 143
Richards, George, 69
Riedesel, Frederick Adolph, 148
Rigbie, Nathaniel, 43

Roberdeau, Daniel, 49, 50, 56, 111–112, 160
Roberdeau, Elizabeth, 111
Robertson, Anne (Lewis), 90
Rodney, Caesar, 20
Rousby, Elizabeth. *See* Plater, Elizabeth
Rumsey, Benjamin, 43–44
Rumsey, Sabina (Blaidenburgh), 43
Rumsey, William, 43
Rush, Benjamin, 26, 79
Rutledge, Sarah. *See* Mathews, Sarah

S

Savage, Elizabeth. *See* Heyward, Elizabeth (Savage)
Schuyler, Philip, 87
Scudder, Joseph, 80
Scudder, Nathaniel, 79–80, 159
Seeley, Mary. *See* Elmer, Mary
Sherman, Elizabeth (Hartwell), 12
Sherman, Rebecca (Prescott), 12
Sherman, Roger, 3, 10, 11–12, 159
Smallwood, William, 43
Smith, James, 113–114
Smith, Jonathan Bayard, 76, 115–116, 160
Smith, Page, 146
Smith, William, 45–46
Spicer, James, 100
Stevenson, George, x
Stevenson, Robert Louis, 100
Stiles, Ezra, 124
Stirling, Lord, 88
Sullivan, John, 97
Swope, Eva, 134

T

Telfair, Edwd, 160
TenBroeck, Christina. *See* Livingston, Christina
Thatcher, John, 54
Thomas, Nicholas, 40
Thomson, Hannah, 71
Thomson, Secretary, 71
Thornburgh, Richard, xi
Trowbridge, Edmund, 123
Trumbull, Jonathan, Jr., 4

Trumbull, Joseph, 4, 62
Trumbull, Mary. *See* Williams, Mary
Twain, Mark, 152

V

Van Cortlant, Pierre, 90
Van Dyke, Nicholas, 160
Van Renssalaer, Stephen, 92
Von Steuben, Baron, 94

W

Walton, Dorothy (Camber), 27
Walton, George, 27–28
Walton, George Hughes, 27
Walton, Jno, 160
Walton, Martha, 27
Ward, Samuel, 123
Warner, Mary. *See* Price, Mary
Washington, George, ix, 4, 34, 42, 53, 56, 58, 62, 88, 90, 94, 97, 107, 108, 109, 110, 112, 119, 120, 122, 124, 128, 130, 134, 146, 148, 149, 150, 153
Weare, Meshech, 72
Wentworth, John, 66, 71–72, 159
Wharton, Thomas, 106, 112
White, Mary. *See* Morris, Mary
Whitfield, George, 131
Wilkinson, James, 68, 76
Wilkinson, William, 100
Williams, Jno, 160
Williams, Mary (Trumbull), 13
Williams, Solomon, 13
Williams, William, 13–14, 98
Willing, Charles, 107
Willing, Thomas, 107
Witherspoon, Ann (Dill), 82
Witherspoon, John, 56, 76, 79, 81–82, 93, 159
Wolcott, Laura (Collins), 15, 16
Wolcott, Oliver, 8, 15–16, 92, 159
Wood, Joseph, 29–30
Worster, General, 114

Y

Yonge, Henry, 27